Helping School Refusing Children and Their Parents

Helping School Refusing Children and Their Parents

A Guide for School-Based Professionals

Christopher A. Kearney

OXFORD
UNIVERSITY PRESS

2008

UNIVERSITY PRESS

Oxford University Press, Inc., publishes works that further
Oxford University's objective of excellence
in research, scholarship, and education.

Oxford   New York
Auckland   Cape Town   Dar es Salaam   Hong Kong   Karachi
Kuala Lumpur   Madrid   Melbourne   Mexico City   Nairobi
New Delhi   Shanghai   Taipei   Toronto

With offices in
Argentina   Austria   Brazil   Chile   Czech Republic   France   Greece
Guatemala   Hungary   Italy   Japan   Poland   Portugal   Singapore
South Korea   Switzerland   Thailand   Turkey   Ukraine   Vietnam

Copyright © 2008 by Oxford University Press, Inc.

Published by Oxford University Press, Inc.
198 Madison Avenue, New York, New York 10016
www.oup.com

Library of Congress Cataloging-in-Publication Data
is available

ISBN: 978-0-19-532024-4

9 8 7 6 5 4 3 2 1

Printed in the United States of America
on acid-free paper

Contents

1

School Refusal Behavior: Definition and Description

Reggie missed the last week of school and cannot seem to get out of bed in the morning. He often cries about having to go to school and seems quite unhappy when there. Reggie mopes around on school nights, especially Sunday nights, and always seems to have stomachaches or headaches before school.

Madison attends school only following a battle with her parents in the morning. She says she does not like school and the people there. Madison complains of having to perform before others at school, such as in gym class, and has skipped several classes this semester that involved a test or presentation.

Brett clings to his mother in the morning before school and refuses to enter the school building. He has run away from school twice in an attempt to get home. On days he is at school, he constantly asks to call his parents. Brett asks the same questions over and over and has pleaded for home schooling.

Gisela has been missing most of school this year. She often skips out after lunch or does not attend school at all. She is not particularly anxious about school but says school is boring and that she would rather be with her friends. Gisela has been fighting a lot with her parents about this issue and is in danger of failing her grade.

Do these cases sound familiar to you? As a school professional, you have likely encountered numerous children or adolescents with trouble attending school or difficulties remaining in classes for an entire day. Youths who miss substantial amounts of school pose one of the most vexing problems for school officials, many of whom are under substantial pressure from administrators, parents, and others to reduce absenteeism. As a clinical child psychologist who has worked with this population for many years as well as with educational professionals at various schools, I know the frustration you feel when trying to get a child back to school. In this book, I hope to share my expertise to help you address this difficult population.

This chapter outlines the purpose of the book, describes the characteristics of youths with school refusal behavior, and provides a model for understanding school refusal behavior and for guiding assessment and intervention.

Purpose of this Book

The purpose of this book is to illuminate the characteristics of youths who refuse to attend school and focus on methods you can use to assess this population and help kids return to school. This book is written primarily for school officials who often address youths with problematic absenteeism. This includes guidance counselors, regular and specialized and special education teachers, principals and deans, school psychologists, school-based social workers, school nurses, school attendance officers, and other relevant personnel. The book may be useful as well when you discuss a child's attendance problem with parents or with professionals such as psychologists, psychiatrists, pediatricians, and others.

This book is part of a short series of books devoted to helping people resolve school refusal behavior. "Step one" in this series is a self-directed book for parents of youths with acute or mild attendance problems (*Getting Your Child to Say "Yes" to School: A Guide for Parents of Youth with School Refusal Behavior;* Oxford University Press, 2007). "Step three" in this series is a set of treatment manuals for psychologists and other clinicians who address severe attendance problems (*When Children Refuse School: A Cognitive-Behavioral Therapy Approach* (2nd ed.) (*Therapist Guide* and *Parent Workbook*); Oxford University Press, 2007). This particular book is "step two" in the series and is designed to help school-based professionals address cases of problematic but *moderate* absenteeism. I do urge you to read the "step one" self-directed book, especially if you recommend that book to parents. The self-directed book is a nice adjunct when you collaborate with parents to resolve a child's school refusal behavior.

What Kinds of Cases Does This Book Cover?

This book is best for *moderate* cases of absenteeism. This means the procedures discussed here may be less necessary for brand-new cases of absenteeism or those that are manageable using simple oversight or increased parental monitoring and guidance. Similarly, the procedures in this book may be less useful for unremitting cases of absenteeism that have lasted many years or involve intense additional problems such as severe learning disorder, depression or bipolar disorder, attention-deficit/ hyperactivity disorder, conduct and aggressive problems, substance abuse, developmental disorder, or psychotic disorder. In these cases, referral to psychological and psychiatric services may be necessary (see box).

This book is also helpful if no *legitimate* reason exists for a child's absenteeism. If a child's attendance problem results from bullying or other real threat to self or property, then the threat must be addressed before using the procedures in this book. Some children continue to refuse school *after* removal of a threat, however, so the procedures in this book may then apply. The focus is on a child's *school attendance* so it is not meant to be used for children who attend school but who experience problems such as classroom disruption, refusal to complete homework, or failure to make friends or participate in class. The following section defines problematic absenteeism and some terms used to describe this population. Later sections discuss characteristics of these youths and present a model that serves as the basis for assessment and intervention recommendations in subsequent chapters.

Problematic Absenteeism and Related Terms

You might be confused by the many terms used to refer to problematic absenteeism. The literature regarding youths with problematic absenteeism is diverse and scattered across disciplines such as education, psychology, social work, criminal justice, and medicine. As such, many different terms for problematic absenteeism have been used. Following is a brief description of terms used in the field as well as the more comprehensive term of *school refusal behavior* used in this book (see also Table 1.1).

Referrals to Mental Health Professionals

For severe cases of school refusal behavior, which may include lengthy problematic absenteeism or intense comorbid problems, I recommend referral to a qualified mental health professional. A *clinical child psychologist* has specialized training with youths with severe behavior problems. A *psychiatrist* is a medical doctor who can prescribe medication for severe behavior problems. For many children with behavior problems that significantly interfere with daily life, seeing a clinical child psychologist *and* a psychiatrist is a good idea. Other mental health professionals who may be helpful to families include social workers and marriage and family therapists.

If you wish to refer a family to a mental health professional in your area, consult with local people knowledgeable about who specializes in certain kinds of problems. Some mental health professionals, for example, have special training in substance abuse or depression. Others work closely with school officials to help resolve problems such as learning disorders, attention-deficit/hyperactivity disorder, or intense school refusal behavior. Ideally, a mental health professional to whom you refer a family for absentee problems should have knowledge of how to treat school refusal behavior and perhaps have access to the "step three" books in this series.

Consulting psychology faculty at a local university is a good start when looking for someone who best fits a family's situation. If you live in an area where this is not possible, contact your state associations of psychologists and psychiatrists. In addition, talk to other professionals at your school who work with certain therapists or who have done so in the past. You may also consult the Web sites of national associations of mental health professionals, such as apa.org, abct.org, and psych.org.

Absenteeism refers to legitimate or illegitimate absence from class or school. Most absences, perhaps around 80%, are *legitimate* and may stem from illness, medical doctor or other professional appointments, family emergencies, religious holidays, poor weather, school-sanctioned release time for work or educational programs, homelessness and other severe family conditions that prevent school attendance or enrollment,

Table 1.1

Absenteeism	Legitimate or illegitimate absence from class or school
School dropout	Premature and permanent departure from school before graduation
School phobia	Fear-based absenteeism
School refusal	Anxiety-based absenteeism
School refusal behavior	Child-motivated refusal to attend school and/or difficulties remaining in classes for an entire day
School withdrawal	Parent-motivated absenteeism
Separation anxiety	Excessive worry and difficulty separating on the part of a child and possibly a parent
Truancy	Illegal absence from school or unexcused absence without parental knowledge

true school-based threats to self or property, and other reasonable or justifiable circumstances. The remaining 20% or so of absences are *illegitimate,* meaning the child does not fully attend school and no reasonable or justifiable circumstances for the absenteeism are present. Illegitimate absenteeism is a primary focus of this book.

Illegitimate absenteeism may be parent- or child-motivated. Parent-motivated absenteeism, when a parent deliberately withholds a child from school, is known as *school withdrawal.* School withdrawal may occur because a parent wants a child home for economic purposes such as babysitting or working to support the family. Other parents keep a child home from school because they have a mental disorder that requires the child's help. Parents with severe anxiety disorders, depression, or substance use, for example, sometimes keep their kids home to help with chores or other basic daily tasks and errands. Parents who maltreat a child may keep him home from school to conceal bruises or other telltale signs of abuse. A parent in a bitter custody battle may be concerned an ex-spouse will kidnap a child before or after school. Parents worry about real and perceived threats at school and may keep a child home for this reason as well. Still other parents pursue unnecessary home schooling. Later chapters refer to instances of parent-based school withdrawal in more detail.

Child-motivated absenteeism, when a child is the driving force behind nonattendance, is referred to by terms such as truancy, school refusal, school phobia, and school dropout. *Truancy* means different things in different school districts and is often defined by a specific number of unexcused absences in a certain time period. The research-based definition of truancy is illegitimate or illegal absence from school without parental knowledge. Truancy has been traditionally linked to delinquent acts such as vandalism, curfew-breaking, or drug use. However, many youths with "truancy" miss school for reasons other than those related to delinquency. The concept of truancy is problematic as well because most parents eventually become aware of their child's attendance problems. In Gisela's case mentioned earlier, she would likely be closest to the traditional concept of truancy, but she demonstrated different behavior problems and fought with her parents about her attendance.

School refusal generally refers to anxiety-based absenteeism. Children with school refusal have difficulties entering or remaining in school and are generally described as fearful, anxious, worried, sad, self-conscious, and timid. Reggie and Madison, the first two cases described at the start of the chapter, are best related to the notion of school refusal. School refusal is often differentiated from truancy because most of these kids are not delinquent. However, great overlap exists among youths traditionally described as truant and those described as having school refusal. Many youths who refuse school show a combination of anxiety-based and acting-out behavior problems.

School refusal is sometimes linked to other, more specific concepts. *School phobia,* for example, refers to fear-based absenteeism, as when a child is specifically afraid of something related to school. Examples include the school bus, fire alarm, or a classroom animal. Such instances are unusual, however, and the term *school phobia* is used less and less in the research literature. In fact, it is best to avoid using this term when consulting with fellow professionals and parents. *Separation anxiety* refers to difficulty of a child, and sometimes a parent, to separate in key situations such as going to school, attending sleepovers, and staying home with a babysitter. Fear and separation anxiety are sometimes components of school refusal.

School dropout refers to premature and permanent departure from school before graduation. According to the National Center for Education Statistics, the status dropout rate for 16- to 24-year-olds in the United States is 10.3%. This rate is somewhat higher for males, Hispanics, lower-income families, employed youths, and youths who have completed 11–12 years of school. Status dropout rates have remained fairly stable in recent years, though one should consider that many youths are never enrolled in school in the first place.

Keeping track of the many terms regarding problematic absenteeism can be quite confusing. This book presents a model for examining *all* youths with problematic absenteeism under *one* rubric called *school refusal behavior*. This term serves as an "umbrella" for those just described and allows for consensus across disciplines. The term *school refusal behavior* has also been linked to a specific way of understanding this population and to the development of assessment and intervention strategies described in this book.

School Refusal Behavior

School refusal behavior refers to child-motivated refusal to attend school or difficulties remaining in classes for an entire day. The term *does not* assume a certain behavioral symptom pattern as do other terms such as truancy (delinquency), school refusal (anxiety), or school phobia (fear). Instead, school refusal behavior simply refers to a collection of different kinds of attendance problems along a spectrum (see Figure 1.1). School refusal behavior excludes school withdrawal or parent-motivated absenteeism (though this book addresses parent-motivated cases in later chapters). Note that school refusal, or anxiety-based absenteeism, is different from the broader term of school refusal behavior.

As shown in Figure 1.1, school refusal behavior refers to different kinds and levels of *obvious absenteeism* (right side of spectrum):

- Some youths are completely absent from school for an extended period of time, perhaps weeks or months.
- Some youths miss only parts of the school year, particularly days following a holiday or other break. Included in this category are youths who may attend school most of the morning but then skip out after lunch.

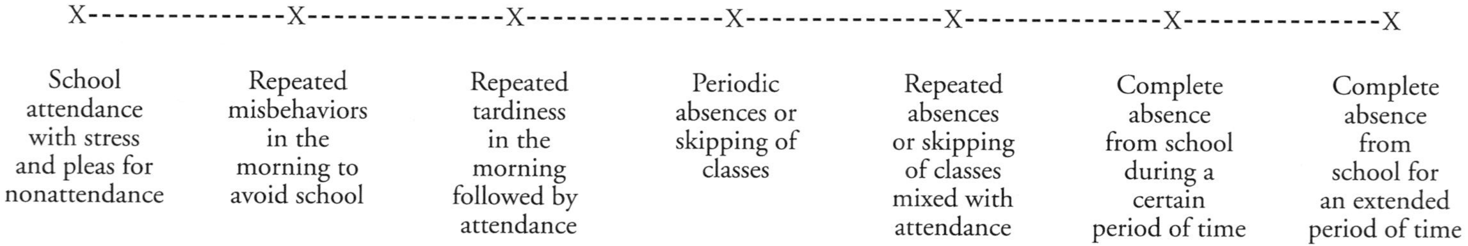

X--------X--------X--------X--------X--------X--------X

| School attendance with stress and pleas for nonattendance | Repeated misbehaviors in the morning to avoid school | Repeated tardiness in the morning followed by attendance | Periodic absences or skipping of classes | Repeated absences or skipping of classes mixed with attendance | Complete absence from school during a certain period of time | Complete absence from school for an extended period of time |

Figure 1.1.

- Some youths repeatedly skip certain classes but attend other classes during the day. Skipped classes often include physical education and those involving performance before others, such as math, choir, band, or English.
- Some youths periodically skip classes or miss school altogether for a day here and a day there. The accumulated absences can eventually trigger a decline in grades and/or citations for excessive absences.

Other children with school refusal behavior may actually be in school most of the time but show misbehavior geared toward nonattendance. The goal of misbehavior is to miss school, but this goal has not yet been reached. School refusal behavior is thus *less obvious* or more subtle. From the left side of the spectrum in Figure 1.1, for example:

- Some youths are chronically tardy or late to school, often following a battle with their parents to avoid school.
- Some youths attend school regularly but show severe behavior problems in the morning, such as from 6:30–8:30 A.M., in an effort to miss school.
- Some youths attend school with significant distress. These youths may cry often and plead with parents and school officials for future nonattendance.

Keep in mind that many youths show *varying patterns* of school refusal behavior, or different points on the spectrum in Figure 1.1, sometimes on a day-to-day basis. Consider, for example, the following case:

Daniel is a 13-year-old boy in middle school who has had attendance problems since fifth grade. His attendance rates have gradually deteriorated over time to the point that Daniel is physically in school only about 60% of the time. During the past week, Daniel skipped school completely on Monday, attended Tuesday morning but not Tuesday afternoon, arrived late to school on Wednesday before staying the entire day, skipped one class on Thursday, and attended school without difficulty on Friday.

From Daniel's case, you can see that degree of absenteeism, or type of school refusal behavior, can shift frequently and even daily. You can also see that Daniel's problems have been ongoing and have worsened over the years. In fact, Daniel occasionally missed school in fifth grade, actively refused to attend school in the morning during sixth grade, and frequently skipped classes in seventh grade prior to his current problems. Cases like Daniel's underscore *the need to monitor a child's level of school refusal on a daily basis* (see Chapter 2). Charting the history and current nature of a child's school refusal behavior is important for understanding the scope of the problem and the level of complexity necessary for an intervention. Chronic cases such as Daniel's, where school refusal behavior lasts longer than one calendar year, will obviously require a much more complex intervention than someone with acute school refusal behavior whose problem has lasted only a few weeks. The following section discusses characteristics of youths with school refusal behavior in greater detail.

Characteristics of Youths with School Refusal Behavior

When you read the cases presented in this chapter, you can see that a key hallmark of youths with school refusal behavior is symptom *heterogeneity.* This means any particular child with school refusal behavior will typically show a wide pattern of covert and overt behavior problems. *Covert behavior problems* are those less obvious and more difficult to identify. Common covert behavior problems in youths with school refusal behavior include general and social anxiety, worry, fear, panic, sadness, fatigue, self-consciousness, and physical complaints such as stomachaches and headaches.

Overt behavior problems are those more obvious and easier to identify. Common overt behavior problems in youths with school refusal behavior include noncompliance and defiance, running away from home or school to avoid attendance, aggression, clinging, temper tantrums, refusal to move, dawdling, crying, hiding, lying, and reassurance-seeking (asking the same questions or making the same statements over and over, usually regarding pleas for nonattendance). Most children with school refusal behavior show various covert *and* overt behavior problems.

How common is school refusal behavior? Very common, as you may well know! If prevalence rates for all the school nonattendance patterns from Figure 1.1 are added, the overall prevalence of school refusal behavior may be as high as 28% (see Kearney, 2001). A recent large-scale community study of youths with school refusal and truancy pegged the prevalence rate at 8.2%, though this did not count youths who attended school with great distress or who did so following morning behavior problems. You can see that the prevalence of school refusal behavior is substantial and actually greater than many major childhood behavior disorders such as depression or attention-deficit/hyperactivity disorder.

Youths may refuse school at any time but do so most commonly at age 10–13 years. This may reflect entry into middle school, a particularly difficult transition for many children, as well as entry into adolescence and increased social and academic stress. School refusal behavior is not closely linked to gender, race, or socioeconomic status, though school dropout rates are more common among males, diverse students, and lower-income families. Longitudinal studies indicate that youths with chronic school refusal behavior are at risk in adulthood for economic, social, marital, and psychiatric problems.

Many researchers have tried to organize youths with school refusal behavior according to the form of their behavior, but this approach has not been largely successful. An alternative method of understanding this population is to examine the *reasons* youths refuse school. This model, which serves as the basis for much of the material in this book, is described next.

A Functional Model of School Refusal Behavior

Why is it that children and adolescents refuse to attend school? The reasons are quite complex and include many contextual variables discussed later in this chapter. For now, I focus on specific rewards or reinforcers that maintain a child's school refusal behavior over time. Knowing these rewards or reinforcers helps us understand what use or *function* school refusal behavior has for a particular child. In other words, we want to know what a particular child is getting out of refusing school. Although evaluating the form of a child's school refusal behavior is important, such as tantrums or skipping class, identifying the function of a child's school refusal behavior will go a long way toward deciding which intervention to use.

There are four main reasons kids refuse school. They are listed here and then described in detail. Note that each reason aligns respectively with the four cases presented at the beginning of the chapter:

- To avoid general school-related distress caused by known or unknown factors.
- To escape aversive social and/or evaluative situations at school.
- To pursue attention from significant others, such as parents.
- To pursue tangible rewards outside of school.

Function 1: Avoiding General School-Related Stress

Jody is a 6-year-old girl who often cries on the playground before school. Jody's parents are usually able to get their daughter dressed in the morning and ready for school but cannot get her to enter the school building when the bell rings at 8:50 A.M. On the playground, Jody cries loudly, throws herself on the ground, and sometimes runs back to her parent's car. Jody says she does not like school but cannot say why. Her parents are frustrated by the fact that Jody has now missed three weeks of school. Oftentimes, Jody's parents take their daughter home after these problems on the playground.

Some youths like Jody refuse school *to avoid general school-related stress.* This applies more to children aged 5–10 years than to adolescents and includes youths who are particularly upset about something related to school. In some cases, a child can identify what stressor causes her to miss school. Examples of stressors in this function include a fire alarm, classroom animal, or school bus. In addition, many youths of this function have difficulties with *transitions.* In other words, they have great difficulty moving from the playground to classroom, from the classroom to the lunchroom, or from the lunchroom to some specialized class. Such difficulty with transition seems to apply to Jody. Many of these children are fine once they finally arrive at a particular place, such as their regular classroom, but they have great difficulty getting to that place initially.

Children in this function, like Jody or Reggie at the beginning of the chapter, often cannot say what specific stressor causes them to miss school. *Do not be overly concerned if a child cannot say specifically why she is not in school.* Many younger children do not have the cognitive ability to describe their emotions or stressors at length or may not truly know what bothers them. Many of these kids have already been asked many times by parents and others why they are not going to school or what bothers them so much. A child's failure to answer this question should not necessarily be viewed as noncompliance or defiance.

Although children of this function show many different behaviors, the following are particularly common:

- Difficulty concentrating in school because of distress.
- Excessive crying or tearfulness.
- Fear of a specific school-related object or situation.

- General anxiety or nervousness.
- In-school behaviors designed to avoid class, such as feigned illness to be sent to a school nurse or disruptive behavior to be sent home.
- Irritability in the form of cranky temperament, muscle tension, or restlessness.
- Ongoing pleas to parents and school officials for a form of home-based instruction.
- Ongoing verbal statements about not wanting to be in school or "hating" school.
- Physical complaints that are often vague in nature, such as stomachaches, headaches, nausea, abdominal pain, and fatigue.
- Pleas for future nonattendance or excused absences.
- Sadness or withdrawal from peers and teachers; sadness or withdrawal may overlap with anxious feelings or behaviors.
- Shaky voice or hands.

These symptoms of distress about school can be generally divided into physical, cognitive, and behavioral components. *Physical components* include bodily symptoms such as shakiness, stomachaches and headaches, and muscle tension. *Cognitive or thinking components* include ongoing questions or statements about having to attend school and other verbal complaints or pleas regarding school attendance and nonattendance. *Behavioral components* include overt symptoms such as crying, withdrawal from others, and difficulty concentrating. These components are often mixed with one another, as in cases like Reggie or Jody.

Physical, cognitive, and behavioral components of distress often progress in a certain sequence or pattern for these youths. Consider Figures 1.2, 1.3, and 1.4, for example. Figure 1.2 shows that a child's physical behaviors may precede certain thoughts (cognitions) that precede certain school refusal behaviors. Figure 1.3 shows that a child's thoughts (cognitions) may precede physical problems that then lead to school refusal behaviors. For other children, physical behaviors may come first and lead to problematic thoughts and physical feelings (Figure 1.4). An important part of assessing these kids is to learn what specific sequence is most pertinent. Chapter 2 describes assessment methods to identify these components and the sequence of behaviors for a particular child.

Keep in mind that this function refers to children not distressed by a true school-based threat or other legitimate reason. If a child is

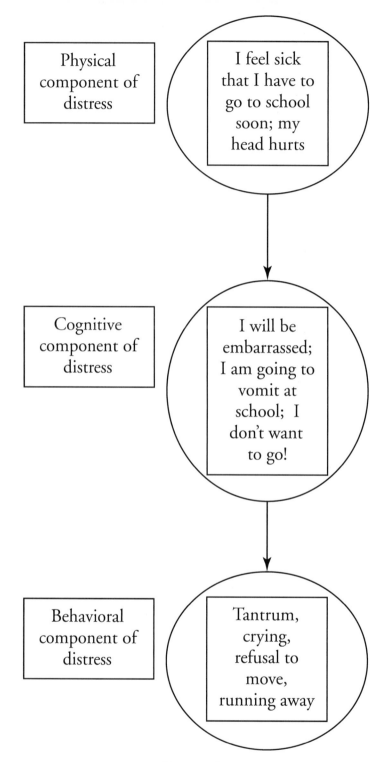

Figure 1.2.

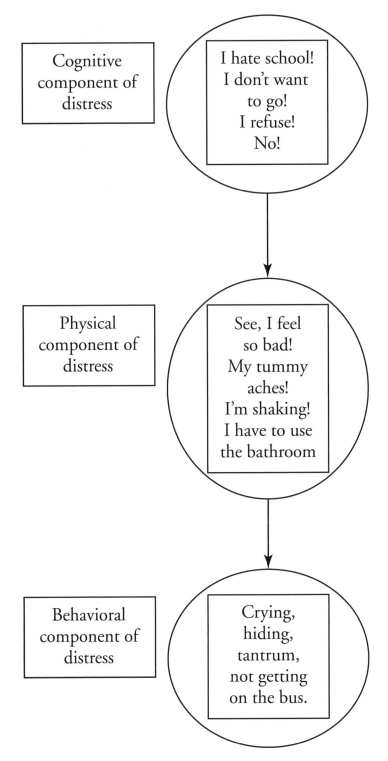

Figure 1.3.

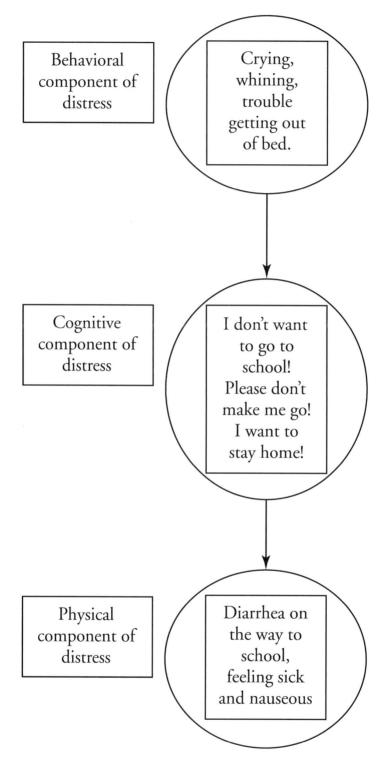

Figure 1.4.

bullied at school or is legitimately afraid of harm to self or personal property, then this situation must be addressed first. This function refers to youths who are much more distressed about school than is justified or understandable. In addition, keep in mind that these children are generally much more concerned about *not being in school* than wanting to be home (see Function 3).

Function 2: Escape from Aversive Social and/or Evaluative Situations

Arya is a 13-year-old boy in eighth grade with great trouble attending classes during the day. Arya is particularly distressed about what others think of him and feels humiliated during performances before others. In particular, Arya is concerned about physical education and math classes, both of which involve solo performance before others. Arya commonly skips certain classes and has occasionally refused to attend school for an entire day.

Some kids, like Arya, are quite distressed about school but *can* identify specific situations that cause them great anxiety. Situations that commonly cause the greatest anxiety are *social or evaluative in nature.* Below are some common *social* situations that bother these kids:

- Answering or speaking on the telephone.
- Asking others for help, particularly people in authority or those a child does not know well.
- Attending assemblies or being among a large group of people.
- Establishing dates or interaction times with friends.
- Interacting with peers in a hallway, playground, cafeteria, or other school-based setting.
- Participating in group meetings or extracurricular activities.
- Starting or maintaining conversations with other kids or adults, particularly those a child does not know well.
- Working or cooperating with others on an academic or other project.

Common *performance* situations that bother these kids include:

- Answering a teacher's question, whether voluntarily or after being solicited.
- Driving before others, as in driver education class.
- Eating among people in a school cafeteria.
- Having one's picture taken.

- Making formal oral presentations before others at school.
- Performing in physical education class.
- Singing or playing a musical instrument before others.
- Speaking or reading before others in class or some other school-based setting.
- Taking tests or completing other graded tasks.
- Undressing before others in a locker room.
- Using restrooms at school.
- Walking into a classroom, hallway, or other school area where many people are present.
- Writing before others, such as solving a math problem on the board.

Youths who refuse school to escape social and/or evaluative situations are typically older (11–17 years) than kids in the first function. Adolescents are more cognitively advanced and can more easily pinpoint specific situations that cause their distress. Many studies indicate that adolescents worry most about school-related situations, especially those involving interactions with others and performance before others. This social and evaluative anxiety overlaps as well with the natural egocentrism that many adolescents experience. When intensified, school refusal behavior can result.

Youths who refuse school to escape aversive social and/or evaluative situations are often anxious when attending school, skip particular classes such as physical education, avoid situations where others are present, ask for course schedule changes or other exemptions, and may not submit homework that is imperfect. In addition, as with Arya, some of these youths skip sections of a school day or miss an entire day. As mentioned earlier, fluctuations in attendance patterns are not unusual.

Many youths who refuse school to escape aversive social and/or evaluative situations also have physical, cognitive, and behavioral components of anxiety discussed for Function 1. In addition, these youths have unique sequences or patterns of physical, cognitive, and behavioral components that lead to school refusal behavior. Because youths of this function are generally *more cognitively advanced,* however, one would expect to see more complex thoughts related to school attendance. Again, this excludes legitimate threats to personal self or property.

Youths who refuse school to (1) avoid general distress or (2) escape aversive social and/or evaluative situations have something in common. Both refuse school for *negative reinforcement.* That is, a child is actively refusing school to avoid or escape something aversive or painful at school. In these cases, the child is not particularly concerned with being home or with friends outside of school (though this may become part of the problem). Instead, something at school or related to school, such as the school bus, creates severe distress for the child. Chapter 3 discusses methods of addressing youths with negatively reinforced school refusal behavior. In contrast, the next two functions involve *positive reinforcement,* or pursuit of rewards outside of school.

Function 3: Pursuit of Attention from Significant Others

Chase is a 7-year-old boy who refuses to attend school without his mother. He insists that his mother either stay in class with him, volunteer as a teacher aide, or eat lunch with him in exchange for his school attendance. Chase's mother initially missed work to be with her son but is now faced with the difficult decision of whether to quit her job, leave Chase's classroom altogether, or place her son in home schooling. Chase's tantrums and screaming in school have become increasingly problematic.

Children like Chase refuse school to *pursue attention from significant others.* "Significant others" typically include parents, and often fathers as well as mothers, but can also include grandparents, siblings, or other caretakers or adults. In cases like Chase and Brett from the beginning of the chapter, the main function or reward is time spent with a parent or significant other. This function differs from the first function. Although the behavior patterns can be similar, children who pursue attention from significant others are not especially anxious or distressed about school-related items or situations. In fact, these children often attend school just fine if only a parent or someone they know well attends with them. If not, then the child's behavior is usually geared toward going home or to a parent's workplace.

Typical behaviors in this function include noncompliance and defiance, tantrums, manipulative and oppositional behavior, stubbornness and resistance, and guilt-inducing behaviors. Complaints of physical symptoms such as headaches and stomachaches are common but no medical cause is usually found. Many of these children expertly manipulate their parents to get what they want. Some prepare for school and then actively refuse just as family members are ready to leave. Others "play dead" or otherwise resist preparing for school to be allowed to stay home.

Children who refuse school for attention tend to be younger, around 5–10 years of age. Attendance patterns in this group are variable. Some youths display intense morning misbehaviors in an effort to miss school, but their parents somehow get them into the school building. Other kids are chronically tardy to school because the morning battle has raged for some time. Still other kids force their parents to acquiesce and take them home or to work. In other cases, like Chase's, parents accommodate a child's request but still require school attendance. Doing so, however, obviously puts parents in a long-term precarious situation, especially if they need to go to work.

Many children who refuse school for attention also display inappropriate in-school behaviors if away from parents. They may badger teachers and others to be sent home, make constant telephone calls to their parents, ask when a parent is scheduled to pick them up after school, ask the same questions or make the same statements repeatedly about having to attend school, become disruptive during the day to be sent home, and even run away from the school building to try to get home. Although many of these kids actually attend school fine once parents get them there, some continue to misbehave to induce nonattendance.

You might be tempted to think of these kids as having separation anxiety, and some do. Indeed, some worry constantly about parents getting into a car accident or having to go to the hospital. However, I am describing a *broader construct* in which a child's general behavior is geared toward receiving attention from parents. As such, the behavior is generally more manipulative and oppositional than it is fear- or anxiety-based. Some overlap with true distress could occur in some cases, however.

Keep in mind that the current focus is on attention-seeking in cases where such behavior is not justified. Other situations exist in which a child's concern for a parent's safety or about who will pick her up after school *is* legitimate. You have likely dealt with children whose parents are in bitter custody disputes, who have suffered a major health or financial problem, or who maltreat their child. In these cases, a child's excessive attention-seeking toward a certain adult may be understandable. In other cases, however, a family's situation has been resolved and a child is still seeking attention inappropriately. Children who refuse school for attention do so for positive reinforcement that often has little to do with the school setting. Following is a discussion of the last function that also involves positively reinforced school refusal behavior:

Function 4: Pursuit of Tangible Rewards Outside of School

Caroline is a 15-year-old student in tenth grade who has missed substantial amounts of school time this year. Caroline often skips school after lunch or sometimes misses an entire day to be with her friends. Although it is unclear what Caroline does when not in school, she says she often eats lunch, cruises the local mall, and attends parties at friends' houses. Caroline's grades have declined sharply in recent weeks and she is in danger of being referred to the juvenile justice system for excessive absences.

Some kids miss school simply because they have more fun outside of school than they do in school. In these cases, youths refuse school to *pursue tangible rewards outside of school*. Tangible rewards refer to specific things or activities a child wants that are available primarily off-campus. In addition to Caroline's activities, examples include sleeping late, watching television, playing videogames, accessing the Internet, riding a bike, joyriding in a car, or working at a job. More dangerous activities could be involved as well, such as drug use or unprotected sexual behavior.

Most youths who refuse school for tangible rewards outside of school are not particularly anxious about attending school, though many claim to be bored when in class. Instead, alluring activities outside of school are powerful draws away from class. Most youths of this function are aged 11–17 years. Many skip school after lunch or miss an entire day or come in late to school. Missing school for these kids is obviously something they wish to keep secret, so parents and even school officials may be unaware for some time that a problem exists. This problem is more serious than the common "senioritis" seen in some adolescents who miss school just prior to graduation when consequences for absenteeism are not overly severe. Instead, I am describing students who miss considerable amounts of school to the extent that their grades and legal status become problematic.

Cases like Caroline and Gisela at the beginning of the chapter are most closely associated with the traditional concept of truancy. However, not all of these kids necessarily show highly delinquent behaviors, and their parents eventually become knowledgeable of the situation. A common characteristic of many of these families, however, is extensive conflict. This is the one function in which family fighting and tension are most likely to be present, especially if legal issues become pertinent. Many school personnel, for example, are more likely to refer a case like Caroline's to a juvenile justice system than a younger child like Jody or Chase.

A particular wrinkle in this function is that youths' complaints about the quality of their education are sometimes legitimate. One can see where it would be difficult to remain in classes for an entire day in a school that is extremely rule-oriented and not highly responsive to the individual educational needs of a student. Boredom at school is a very common complaint among these youths and helps explain many cases of dropout. When assessing youths who may be pursuing tangible rewards outside of school, special attention should be paid to parent and student complaints about the general school climate (see also Chapter 7).

Multiple Functions

Children may also refuse school for more than one function. This scenario is especially common in cases that have lasted for some time. A common example is a child so distressed about school that parents allow him to stay home a few days. The child then realizes the fun things he can do while home and begins to refuse school to avoid distress *and* to pursue tangible rewards outside of school (functions 1 *and* 4). Another common example is a child out of school for a long period of time, perhaps to seek attention or tangible rewards, who then becomes nervous at the prospect of having to return to school and face new peers and teachers and mounds of makeup work.

Youths who refuse school for more than one reason or function require a more detailed and complex intervention than youths who refuse school for just one function. Likewise, youths who miss school for longer periods of time require more complex interventions than youths just starting to miss school. Interventions with this population also become more complicated when broader problems exist. Some of these broader problems that could impact a child's school refusal behavior are described next.

Contextual Variables

> Surya is a 16-year-old in eleventh grade who has missed much of the last three months of school. Contact with parents about this problem has been sporadic and not productive. Surya says his family has been experiencing severe financial problems and that his parents are more concerned with finding jobs than monitoring his school attendance. In addition, Surya complains that school is boring and that his teachers are more concerned with their own safety in large classrooms than teaching students. He has talked about dropping out of school to work and later pursue an equivalency diploma.

Until now, this chapter has focused on specific variables or functions related to school refusal behavior in children and adolescents. Focusing on these functions will help you address different cases of problematic absenteeism. However, psychological factors such as the ones discussed here are not the only ones that contribute to school refusal behavior. Indeed, broader variables must be considered to fully understand the context of any child's school refusal behavior, especially in cases like Surya's. *Contextual variables* are broad environmental events that indirectly affect a child's behavior. Contextual variables most closely related to problematic absenteeism are introduced in this section and discussed more thoroughly in Chapter 7.

Homelessness, for example, is a significant barrier to school attendance for many children. School districts commonly require immunization and academic records, birth certificates, permanent home addresses, and proof of guardianship just for enrollment. Families who are homeless also commonly lack the ability to transport a child to school, purchase clothing and school supplies, or even maintain residence in a particular school zone. Closely linked to homelessness, of course, is *poverty.* Children of impoverished families are much more likely to miss school and drop out of school than their peers. A family's need for additional income is obviously a primary motivating factor for excessive absenteeism in some adolescents.

Another important contextual factor is *teenage pregnancy.* Teenage mothers on average complete about two fewer school years than their peers and are much less likely to complete high school. Many teenage mothers leave school once the baby is born, though some researchers have found that alternative educational programs post-pregnancy can help reduce school absenteeism and dropout (see Chapter 7).

Still another key contextual variable is *school violence and victimization.* School violence and victimization obviously involves a broad spectrum of threats that range from bullying to robbery to assault. Students subjected to bullying and other forms of violence are much more likely than peers to avoid school activities and miss school out of fear of attack or harm. Such avoidance is often related to whether a student has been victimized in the past. Violence at school can also be a reason some parents allow a child to remain home from school.

School climate has also received attention with respect to school absenteeism. *School climate* generally refers to student feelings of connectedness to their school and degree of support a student feels for academic and other needs. The construct also includes school safety, positive classroom management, participation in extracurricular activities, and flexible or tolerant disciplinary practices. Researchers have found school climate to be significantly related to school attendance and lower school dropout. As one might expect, positive school climate is related to less school violence and victimization as well. Conversely, poor school climate can be related to inadequate attention to a student's needs and boredom at school, which is a key reason many adolescents leave school prematurely.

Parent involvement is obviously another important contextual variable regarding school attendance. Parent involvement includes such things as attending parent-teacher conferences, checking homework and engaging in reading, limiting television, becoming active in the development of a child's school, and monitoring school attendance. Reasons for poor parent involvement, which can lead to chronic absenteeism, include cultural variables such as concern about assimilation, language barriers, relaxed attitudes about academic achievement, and mistrust of school officials. However, several school-based problems can contribute to poor parent involvement as well. These include extensive school official-parent conflict, teacher absenteeism, lack of communication about a child's school attendance, and low teacher expectations.

Other contextual variables that contribute to a child's absenteeism include chaotic or otherwise problematic family dynamics and conflict, divorce, residence in unsafe neighborhoods, poor supervision, and maltreatment. Finally, chronic illness and medical conditions can obviously impact a child's school attendance. One of the leading causes of absenteeism worldwide is asthma and related respiratory conditions. Indeed, children with asthma miss 1.5–3.0 times more school days than youths without asthma. Other conditions closely related to school absenteeism include cancer, chronic pain, epilepsy, gastrointestinal problems, headache, head lice, influenza, injury, menstrual problems, obesity, orodental disease, recovery from surgical or other medical procedures, and type 1 diabetes, among others. Absenteeism has also been linked to indoor pollutants and poor air ventilation as well as risky health behaviors such as illicit alcohol and other drug use, unprotected sexual behavior, suicide attempt, and poor nutrition.

Final Comments and What's Next

School refusal behavior is a common but complex and difficult problem that can lead to serious consequences for a child. The first step in addressing a child with school refusal behavior is to fully understand the forms and function of the behavior as well as contextual variables that may contribute to the behavior. In Chapter 2, assessment methods for this population are discussed, with a particular emphasis on key questions you can ask as well as other time-efficient methods of data collection. Chapter 3 outlines recommended procedures for youths with negatively reinforced school refusal behavior, and Chapter 4 outlines recommended procedures for youths with positively reinforced school refusal behavior.

Later chapters involve a discussion of larger issues. Chapter 5 includes suggestions for addressing difficult parents and problematic family dynamics in this population. A description of other special topics related to functions of school refusal behavior is presented as well. Chapter 6 outlines strategies to prevent relapse in individual cases of school refusal behavior as well as systemic strategies to prevent and address this population. Chapter 7 revisits contextual variables that impact school refusal behavior and provides specific suggestions for school-based personnel.

2

Assessing Cases of School Refusal Behavior

Olivia is a 9-year-old student in fourth grade who, since the beginning of September, often cries before entering school and is sometimes taken home by her parents. On days she does attend school, Olivia is frequently late to class or cries loudly in her classroom. Her teacher complains that Olivia's sobbing becomes disruptive to the point that she must sit outside the classroom. Olivia commonly asks to go to the bathroom or nurse's office or to call her mother. She says she does not like school but cannot identify anything in particular that upsets her while there.

Luke is a 16-year-old student in high school who has missed considerable amounts of school time this year. Luke commonly leaves school after lunch and has registered 10 complete absences by mid-February. He complains that school is boring and he is often tempted by friends to miss school. Although Luke is fairly bright, his grades have declined to the point that he may fail the academic year. Luke's parents have constantly fought with their son about this issue but are becoming more discouraged and less motivated to change the situation. School officials have considered whether to refer Luke and his parents to the juvenile justice system for truancy and educational neglect.

School officials are commonly faced with cases like Olivia and Luke every day. Chapter 1 talked about the different aspects of school refusal behavior as well as a model for understanding this population based on what reinforces the behavior. This chapter outlines methods of assessing kids like Olivia and Luke. Some of these methods are less time intensive for school officials with little opportunity for conducting a detailed assessment. Other methods *are* time intensive and might be under the purview of someone who can conduct a detailed assessment, such as a school-based social worker or school psychologist.

This chapter begins with a discussion of basic and less time-intensive methods that *must be part of any assessment for a youth with school refusal behavior.* These methods include daily monitoring of attendance and behavior as well as discussions with the student and parents. Worksheets, a questionnaire regarding the function of school refusal behavior, and specific recommendations for interview questions comprise this section. Later in the chapter, more time-intensive assessment methods are described. These methods include behavioral observation, other questionnaires, review of records, and formal testing.

Less Time-Intensive Assessment Methods

Several assessment methods for youths with school refusal behavior are essential and take little time to do. The methods in this section will help you collect information about day-to-day fluctuations in a child's school refusal behavior, forms of school refusal behavior such as tantrums or level of distress, and primary reasons a child is refusing school. These methods involve a *concentrated behavioral assessment approach* designed to measure the specific "nuts and bolts" of a child's daily behavior. In particular, this chapter covers daily monitoring of attendance and behavior, a questionnaire for assessing the function of a child's school refusal behavior, and interview questions.

Why are these assessment methods necessary? Three key questions must be answered when addressing cases of school refusal behavior:

- What is the form of a child's school refusal behavior?
- What is the function of a child's school refusal behavior?
- What is the best intervention for this child?

Forms of behavior refer to *exactly what a child does* as he refuses school. Common symptoms of school refusal behavior were listed in Chapter 1, but particularly frequent examples include those mentioned earlier for Olivia and Luke. Crying, temper tantrums, avoidance, attention-seeking behavior, and leaving a school campus are all symptoms you have likely seen in these cases. Functions of behavior refer to *rewards that maintain a child's school refusal behavior over time.* We must know *why* a particular child is refusing school. Finally, of course, we must understand forms and functions of behavior to establish the best remedial action. The sections that follow cover some specific and less time-intensive assessment methods for this population that will allow you to examine forms and functions of school refusal behavior.

Daily Monitoring of Behavior and Attendance

Youths who refuse school fluctuate greatly in their behaviors and attendance patterns. In addition, many youths miss school because their actual attendance is not well documented by parents, school officials, or others. Parent-school official communication often suffers as a result in these situations as well, which leads to conflict or delay when addressing an absentee problem. For children with problematic absenteeism, I recommend *establishing a daily monitoring system* to collect information about a child's behavior and attendance.

Parents are obviously a preferred option for collecting data on child behavior and attendance, though some parents may not be up to this task. For this reason, worksheets (see Worksheet 2.1 and 2.2) that can be given to parents or modified so you or someone at your school can collect available information are provided here. Worksheet 2.1 is fairly basic and covers the number of hours a particular child is in school and whether an absence that day was legitimate or illegitimate. Each school district has its own policies that define legitimate school attendance, but some common reasons, such as illness or weather, were listed in Chapter 1.

Worksheet 2.2 is a little more complex and covers the level of distress a child shows during a school day. Again, ideally, parents and the child should complete this form, especially because they can provide ratings for mornings, evenings, and weekends. Failing this, however, a school official who knows the child could provide morning or afternoon distress ratings if the child attends school for at least part of the day. The worksheet will obviously not apply to youths completely absent from school or who have no distress about attending school. Most youths of this population, however, such as Olivia, show some level of distress.

Alternative worksheets are also provided (see Worksheets 2.3 and 2.4). Worksheet 2.3 represents a daily report card that can be completed by a teacher or other knowledgeable school official and sent home to parents each day. This worksheet is brief but informative enough that

Worksheet 2.1

	Number of Hours Spent in School	*Legitimate Absence?*
Monday	_____	_____
Tuesday	_____	_____
Wednesday	_____	_____
Thursday	_____	_____
Friday	_____	_____
Monday	_____	_____
Tuesday	_____	_____
Wednesday	_____	_____
Thursday	_____	_____
Friday	_____	_____
Monday	_____	_____
Tuesday	_____	_____
Wednesday	_____	_____

Thursday _____ _____

Friday _____ _____

Monday _____ _____

Tuesday _____ _____

Wednesday _____ _____

Thursday _____ _____

Friday _____ _____

Monday _____ _____

Tuesday _____ _____

Wednesday _____ _____

Thursday _____ _____

Friday _____ _____

What time should the child enter school in the morning? _____

What time should the child leave school in the afternoon? _____

Worksheet 2.2

	Adult Rating of Child's Distress			Child's Rating of His/Her Distress		
	Morning	Afternoon	Evening	Morning	Afternoon	Evening
Monday						
Tuesday						
Wednesday						
Thursday						
Friday						
Saturday						
Sunday						
Monday						
Tuesday						
Wednesday						
Thursday						
Friday						
Saturday						
Sunday						
Monday						
Tuesday						
Wednesday						

Thursday

Friday

Saturday

Sunday

Monday

Tuesday

Wednesday

Thursday

Friday

Saturday

Sunday

Monday

Tuesday

Wednesday

Thursday

Friday

Saturday

Sunday

X——X——X——X——X——X——X——X——X——X——X					
0 1 2 3 4 5 6 7 8 9 10					
None	A little	Some	Stronger	A lot	The worst

Worksheet 2.3

Daily Report Card

Date: _____

Number of hours spent in school today _____

Level of distress shown by child today (use 0–10 scale) _____

X——X——X——X——X——X——X——X——X——X——X

0	1	2	3	4	5	6	7	8	9	10
None		A little		Some		Stronger		A lot		The worst

Behavior problems in school today

_____

_____

_____

_____

_____

_____

_____

_____

Homework today or other comments

_____

_____

_____

_____

_____

_____

_____

_____

_____

Worksheet 2.4

	Monday	Tuesday	Wednesday	Thursday	Friday
Week 1					
Refuses/cannot get out of bed	____	____	____	____	____
Refuses to move	____	____	____	____	____
Will not get ready for school	____	____	____	____	____
Locks self in room or car	____	____	____	____	____
Cries a lot	____	____	____	____	____
Temper tantrum	____	____	____	____	____
Excessive dawdling	____	____	____	____	____
Clings to an adult	____	____	____	____	____
Stomachache or other complaint	____	____	____	____	____
Runs away from home or school	____	____	____	____	____
_____	____	____	____	____	____
(Other)					
_____	____	____	____	____	____
(Other)					
Week 2					
Refuses/cannot get out of bed	____	____	____	____	____
Refuses to move	____	____	____	____	____
Will not get ready for school	____	____	____	____	____
Locks self in room or car	____	____	____	____	____
Cries a lot	____	____	____	____	____

Temper tantrum   ___   ___   ___   ___   ___

Excessive dawdling   ___   ___   ___   ___   ___

Clings to an adult   ___   ___   ___   ___   ___

Stomachache or
    other complaint   ___   ___   ___   ___   ___

Runs away from home
    or school   ___   ___   ___   ___   ___

_____   ___   ___   ___   ___   ___

(Other)

_____   ___   ___   ___   ___   ___

(Other)

Week 3

Refuses/cannot get
    out of bed   ___   ___   ___   ___   ___

Refuses to move   ___   ___   ___   ___   ___

Will not get ready
    for school   ___   ___   ___   ___   ___

Locks self in room
    or car   ___   ___   ___   ___   ___

Cries a lot   ___   ___   ___   ___   ___

Temper tantrum   ___   ___   ___   ___   ___

Excessive dawdling   ___   ___   ___   ___   ___

Clings to an adult   ___   ___   ___   ___   ___

Stomachache or
    other complaint   ___   ___   ___   ___   ___

Runs away from home
    or school   ___   ___   ___   ___   ___

_____   ___   ___   ___   ___   ___

(Other)

_____   ___   ___   ___   ___   ___

(Other)

parents can know immediately what problems their child had that day and, ideally, administer consequences as a result (see Chapter 4). Some school districts or teachers have their own daily report cards, of course, which may replace, supplement, or be combined with information from Worksheet 2.3.

Finally, Worksheet 2.4 is a checklist of common symptoms of school refusal behavior that can be logged each school day. The worksheet covers a 3-week period and may be completed by parents or a knowledgeable school official. The worksheet also includes blank lines so you or parents can list behaviors specific to a child that are not covered by the other symptoms.

Feel free to photocopy each of these worksheets from the book or download multiple copies from the companion Web site at www.oup.com/us/ schoolrefusal. These worksheets only represent examples of what you could supply to parents or complete yourself to obtain baseline information about the forms of a child's school refusal behavior. The worksheets can, of course, be modified to fit your preferences and time constraints. In addition, you may choose to use only one or two of these forms and not all of them. Whatever forms you decide to use, however, it is important that you gather daily information about a child's specific behaviors and attendance patterns. Information about the function of a child's school refusal behavior is important as well, and a tool for measuring this construct is discussed next.

School Refusal Assessment Scale-Revised

Another important tool that can be part of a less time-intensive assessment is the *School Refusal Assessment Scale-Revised,* or SRAS-R. The SRAS-R is a questionnaire to measure the relative strength of each of the four functions of school refusal behavior described in Chapter 1. The SRAS-R is available in child and parent versions (see Appendix 1, Assessment Measures, for copies). Each version of the SRAS-R contains 24 items, six of which are devoted to each of the four functions described in Chapter 1:

- Avoidance of school-related stimuli provoking negative affectivity (combination of anxiety and depression) or general distress (ANA) (items 1, 5, 9, 13, 17, and 21)
- Escape from aversive social and/or evaluative situations (ESE) (items 2, 6, 10, 14, 18, and 22)
- Attention-getting behavior (AGB) (items 3, 7, 11, 15, 19, and 23)

- Pursuit of tangible rewards outside of school (PTR) (items 4, 8, 12, 16, 20, and 24)

Each SRAS-R item is scored on a 0–6 scale from "never" to "always." For the first function, children and parents are asked how often a child refuses school because of bad feelings related to something at school. For the second function, children and parents are asked how often a child refuses school because of difficulties interacting with or performing before others at school. For the third function, children and parents are asked how often a child refuses school to spend time with parents. For the fourth function, children and parents are asked how often a child misses school to have more fun outside of school.

Administration of the SRAS-R is straightforward. Ask the child and parent(s) to separately complete their version of the scale, which should take only a few minutes. This may even be done over the telephone or via e-mail. For young children or those with learning disorders, reading the questions may be necessary. Ideally, SRAS-R ratings are obtained from the child, mother, and father if all are available.

Following completion of each questionnaire, obtain item means for each function. On the SRAS-R-C and each SRAS-R-P, therefore, scores are added as follows:

- Items 1, 5, 9, 13, 17, and 21 (first function).
- Items 2, 6, 10, 14, 18, and 22 (second function).
- Items 3, 7, 11, 15, 19, and 23 (third function).
- Items 4, 8, 12, 16, 20, and 24 (fourth function).

These four total scores are then each divided by 6 (or number of items answered in each set). For example,

- If a child's total rating score across the first item set was 18, then the item mean would be 3.00.
- If a child's total rating score across the second item set was 12, then the item mean would be 2.00.
- If a child's total rating score across the third item set was 36, then the item mean would be 6.00.
- If a child's total rating score across the fourth item set was 6, then the item mean would be 1.00.

Do this separately for ratings from the child, mother, and father.

After this is done, compute the mean item scores per functional condition across all SRAS-R versions given. Let's assume, for example, the following:

- The child's mean item scores from the SRAS-C were 3.00, 3.50, 6.00, and 0.50.
- The mother's mean item scores from the SRAS-P were 4.00, 4.50, 5.50, and 1.00.
- The father's mean item scores from the SRAS-P were 3.50, 4.50, 5.00, and 1.50.

In this case, therefore, the

- Overall mean for the first function would be 3.50 (3.00 + 4.00 + 3.50/3).
- Overall mean for the second function would be 4.17 (3.50 + 4.50 + 4.50/3).
- Overall mean for the third function would be 5.50 (6.00 + 5.50 + 5.00/3).
- Overall mean for the fourth function would be 1.00 (0.50 + 1.00 + 1.50/3).

The highest scoring function is considered to be the primary reason a particular child refuses school. Scores within 0.50 points of one another are considered equivalent. In this case, therefore, the highest scoring function is the third one, or attention-seeking (5.50). If another function were scored at 5.25, for example, that function would be considered equivalent to the attention-seeking function.

You can also evaluate item means for each function as part of a *profile*. In this case, for example, the child may be refusing school somewhat for the first and second functions (i.e., avoidance of stimuli provoking negative affectivity/general distress and escape from aversive social and/or evaluative situations; 3.50 and 4.17). However, the relative influence of the fourth functional condition, tangible rewards, is low (1.00) and may not be a substantial factor.

These figures are hypotheses based on child and parent ratings. Do not assume only from use of the SRAS-R that you know why a child refuses school. Information from the scale must be used in conjunction with information from daily worksheets, interviews, observations, and other methods. In addition, note inconsistencies between child/parent SRAS-R ratings and interview information. In some cases, re-administering the SRAS-R is warranted. In other cases, interviews with relevant family members are needed to resolve discrepancies. Let's turn next to the interview process.

Interview

Interviewing a child refusing to attend school, and his parents, is important to gathering information about attendance patterns and the forms and function of school refusal behavior. It is best to ask questions that surround the four functional conditions described in Chapter 1 and represented on the SRAS-R. This is important especially if discrepancies exist between child and parent reports. In some cases, items from the SRAS-R can be used in interview format if necessary. Offshoot questions from these items are encouraged as well so your inquiries are best tailored to a particular case.

The time you have to devote to a question-and-answer session with parents is likely quite limited, so a list of recommended questions is provided here for your use. These questions are broad and designed to help you gather information about the forms and function of a child's school refusal behavior:

- What are the child's specific forms of absenteeism, and how do these forms change daily?
- How did the child's school refusal behavior develop over time?
- What is the child's level of anxiety or misbehavior upon entering school or in the morning before school?
- What specific school-related stimuli, if they can be identified, provoke the child's concern about going to school?
- Is the child's refusal to attend school legitimate or understandable in some way (see contextual risk factors in Chapter 1)?
- What family disruption or conflict has occurred as a result of a child's school refusal behavior?
- What is the child's academic status?
- Have recent or traumatic home or school events occurred to influence a child's school refusal behavior?
- Are symptoms of school refusal behavior evident on weekends and holidays?
- Are there any non–school-related situations where anxiety or attention-seeking behavior occurs?
- What specific social and/or evaluative situations at school are avoided?
- Is the child willing to attend school if a parent accompanies her?
- What specific tangible rewards does the child pursue outside of school that causes him to miss school?

- Is the child willing to attend school if incentives were provided for attendance?
- Is the child currently seeing a therapist?
- Is the child on, or eligible for, a 504 plan or individualized education plan?
- How much school attendance can the child tolerate (e.g., standing on the playground, sitting in the lobby, going to one class, attending a half day)?

These questions are specifically designed for parents and possibly youths. In some cases, of course, interviews are not feasible. If not, then try to answer the questions yourself using daily monitoring, the SRAS-R, inquiries with colleagues at your school, observations, review of records, and other assessment methods. Keep in mind that sources other than parents can provide you with important information; examples include grandparents, peers, and dating partners. These less time-intensive methods should give you a decent snapshot of a child's forms and function of school refusal behavior. If resources exist for more time-intensive assessment methods to enhance the evaluation process, then I recommend utilizing the methods described next.

More Time-Intensive Assessment Methods

As a school official, your time is likely very limited. That is why this chapter describes assessment methods that require as little time as possible but still provide valuable information about the forms and function of a child's school refusal behavior. The sections that follow describe assessment methods that are more time-intensive and might be more feasible for someone with time to conduct a detailed assessment. These methods include behavioral observation, questionnaires and checklists, reviewing records, and formal testing.

Behavioral Observation

Behavioral observation involves watching a child and her parents in a natural setting, such as a home or playground, to get information about forms and function of behavior. This assessment method is time

Behavioral Observation for School Refusal Behavior

CHILD'S NAME: _____

DATE: _____

Needed: Stopwatch, daily logbook forms
Instructions for the recorder (FOLLOW THESE INSTRUCTIONS STEP BY STEP):
Prior to the home visit, discuss the 0–10 rating scale with the child and parents. Describe in detail the constructs of negative affectivity (i.e., general negative mood including anxiety and depression) and noncompliance (i.e., refusal to comply with parental commands/requests). Distribute to each party a copy of the daily logbook form for review.

Schedule a time to meet with the family in their home setting on a school day. Determine the child's rising time (e.g., 6:30 A.M.) and schedule to arrive 15 minutes earlier. Using a stopwatch, record the amount of time the child resists activities that serve to prepare her for school attendance.

Specifically, record time in minutes taken for the following:

(1) *Verbal/physical resistance to rise from bed at the prespecified time.*
Verbal/physical resistance in this situation is defined as any verbalization, vocalization, or physical behavior that contradicts school attendance. In this situation, such behaviors might include (but are not limited to) verbal and physical noncompliance, clinging to bed, locking oneself in a bedroom, or refusal to move.

(2) *Verbal/physical resistance to dressing, washing, and eating.*
Verbal/physical resistance in this situation is defined as any verbalization, vocalization, or physical behavior that contradicts school attendance. In this situation, such behaviors might include (but are not limited to) verbal and physical noncompliance, clinging, screaming, crying, throwing objects, aggressive behavior, locking oneself in a room, running away, or refusal to move.

(3) *Verbal/physical resistance to riding in a car/bus to school.*
Verbal/physical resistance in this situation is defined as any verbalization,

vocalization, or physical behavior that contradicts school attendance. In this situation, such behaviors might include (but are not limited to) verbal and physical noncompliance, locking oneself in the car, screaming, crying, aggressive behavior, running away, or refusal to move.

(4) *Verbal/physical resistance to entering the school building.*
Verbal/physical resistance in this situation is defined as any verbalization, vocalization, or physical behavior that contradicts school attendance. In this situation, such behaviors might include (but are not limited to) verbal and physical noncompliance, clinging, screaming, crying, aggressive behavior, running away, or refusal to move.

In addition, record the child's rating of negative affectivity on the 0–10 scale where 0 = none, 2 = mild, 4 = moderate, 6 = marked, 8 = severe, and 10 = extreme. Use any number 0–10. REMIND THE CHILD TO USE THE ENTIRE RANGE OF RATINGS.
Record this rating twice:
(1) In the middle of morning preparation activities.
(2) Upon entering the school building (if applicable).

In addition, record the parent's rating of child negative affectivity and noncompliance on the 0–10 scale where 0 = none, 2 = mild, 4 = moderate, 6 = marked, 8 = severe, and 10 = extreme. Use any number 0–10. REMIND THE PARENT TO USE THE ENTIRE RANGE OF RATINGS.
Record this rating twice:
(1) In the middle of morning preparation activities.
(2) Upon entering the school building (if applicable).

Contact the school attendance officer at the child's school to record any time missed that school day. Complete all remaining sections of the recording sheet for the behavioral approach test.

Recording Sheet for Behavioral Observation

PARTICIPANTS: _____

DATE/TIME: _____

1. Record total verbal/physical resistance time for rising from bed:
   TOTAL MINUTES: _____
2. Record total verbal/physical resistance time for dressing, washing, and eating:
   TOTAL MINUTES: _____
3. Record child rating (0–10) of negative affectivity at midpoint of morning preparation activities:
   RATING: _____
4. Record parent rating (0–10) of child's (a) negative affectivity and (b) noncompliance at midpoint of morning preparation activities:
   NEGATIVE AFFECTIVITY RATING: _____
   NONCOMPLIANCE RATING: _____
5. Record total verbal/physical resistance time for riding in a car or bus to school:
   TOTAL MINUTES: _____
6. Record total verbal/physical resistance time for entering the school building:
   TOTAL MINUTES: _____
7. Record child rating (0–10) of negative affectivity upon entering school building (if applicable):
   RATING: _____
8. Record parent rating (0–10) of child's (a) negative affectivity and (b) noncompliance upon entering school building (if applicable):
   NEGATIVE AFFECTIVITY RATING: _____
   NONCOMPLIANCE RATING: _____
9. Record total amount of time missed during the school day:
   TOTAL MINUTES: _____
10. Record total amount of resistance time plus time missed during the school day:
    TOTAL MINUTES: _____
11. Record total time between rising time and end of school day:
    TOTAL MINUTES: _____
12. Calculate percentage of resistance/missed time to total time between rising time and end of school day:
    PERCENTAGE: _____

intensive because, ideally, we want to watch a child long enough to fully understand the absentee problem and what maintains the problem. In other words, we want a good sample of behavior. For our purposes, behavioral observations are described in one of two ways: systematic and less systematic.

Systematic behavioral observations involve a set protocol when a school official schedules a time to watch a child and record specific information about observed behaviors. "Step three" of the school refusal series as described in Chapter 1—the treatment manual for clinicians—describes a systematic method of behavior observation. The protocol and recording sheet for this systematic behavioral observation technique are shown here.

Following parental consent, this systematic observation begins at a child's home early in the morning and proceeds throughout a school day. The observation is heavily weighted toward resistance on a child's part to attend school in the morning, so the observation may not apply to older youths who attend school fine in the morning but skip school later in the day. The protocol lists specific behaviors of interest, such as noncompliance, screaming, locking oneself in a car, and refusal to move. I strongly encourage you to also observe and record *parental reactions* to a child's misbehavior, especially acquiescence and aggression. As an observer, you simply watch and make ratings and recordings of behavior on the sheet provided.

You can use information from the systematic behavioral observation to help you understand the forms of a child's school refusal behavior and develop an opinion about why the behavior continues to occur. You may notice, for example, that a child is generally ignored by parents when appropriately preparing for school but given much attention during a temper tantrum. In this case, the child's school refusal behavior may be attention based. In another case, you may see that a child's parents act appropriately but just cannot get an obviously distressed child to school. This may indicate an anxiety-based problem.

This kind of systematic behavioral observation obviously requires a lot of your time and energy. Another problem with this kind of assessment is that people you are watching may behave differently from their normal behavior if they know you are there. An alternative approach, therefore, is a *less systematic behavioral observation*. In this approach, your observations are more school based and usually shorter.

You may or may not make formal recordings of behavior but instead note important aspects of child and parent behavior that may be helpful for developing an intervention. Examples of less systematic behavioral observations include:

- Standing on the playground in the morning just before the bell rings to watch a child interact with her parent and anxiously resist entering the school building.
- Watching a child interact with peers and adults and perform before others.
- Noting a child's attention-seeking behavior during the school day, such as calling parents often or demanding that a parent attend class.
- Observing a child during a high-risk time for skipping school, such as immediately after lunch.
- Asking teachers and others to supply you with reports about their observations of specific events such as transitions between classes, oral presentations, or participation in physical education class.

Less systematic observations can also occur as you interview a child and his parents in your office. Children who are nervous and upset may be avoiding school-based stimuli that provoke distress. Children who refuse to be interviewed alone might have intense social anxiety. Children who cling tightly to a parent might be refusing school to pursue parent attention. Older youths who vociferously argue with parents to maintain the status quo may be refusing school to pursue tangible rewards outside of school. No "cookbook" strategy exists to know exactly what observed behaviors indicate a particular function of school refusal behavior. You must use your best judgment and supplement your observations with information from other methods described in this chapter. Still, you should watch for aspects of general distress, social and performance anxiety, attention-seeking behavior, and behavior designed to pursue tangible rewards outside of school.

Another less systematic but useful behavioral observation is to assess how close a child can come to full-time school attendance. Many youths, for example, tell me they would go to school if they could only attend two or three classes or even just lunch. In other cases, children can make it to the school lobby but no further. Other children are content to sit in the school library all day without attending class. I recommend discovering the extent to which a child is willing to attend school. *This could then serve as your baseline of behavior and the minimum expectation you have for school attendance.* In the case of Olivia, for example, one might find her willing to begin her day at 10:00 A.M. and that she can attend the rest of the day without difficulty. Her parents could then be asked to bring Olivia to school at that time and then gradually add more classroom time as Olivia successfully manages her anxiety (see Chapter 4).

Questionnaires and Checklists

Many questionnaires and checklists are available commercially to assess behaviors related to school refusal behavior. Child-based self-report measures generally involve ratings of internalizing or covert problems such as general and social anxiety, worry, fear, depression, distress, low self-esteem, and irrational thoughts. Among youths with school refusal behavior, assessing general and social anxiety and depression is particularly important. Below are five commonly used and psychometrically strong measures of these constructs:

- *Multidimensional Scale for Children,* a 39-item scale that measures harm avoidance and physical anxiety, separation/panic, and social anxiety.
- *Screen for Child Anxiety-Related Disorders,* a 41-item scale that measures somatic/panic symptoms, general anxiety, separation anxiety, social anxiety, and school-related fear.
- *Social Anxiety Scale for Children-Revised* and *Social Anxiety Scale for Adolescents,* which are 26-item scales of social anxiety that measure fear of negative evaluation from peers, social avoidance and distress specific to new situations, and generalized social avoidance and distress.
- *Social Phobia and Anxiety Inventory for Children,* a 26-item scale of social anxiety that contains items surrounding assertiveness, general conversation, physical and cognitive symptoms, avoidance, and public performance.
- *Children's Depression Inventory,* a 27-item scale that measures negative mood, interpersonal problems, ineffectiveness, anhedonia, and negative self-esteem.

Parent- and teacher-based questionnaires and checklists cover internalizing and externalizing behavior problems. Several are commonly used and have excellent psychometric strength:

- *Child Behavior Checklist* and *Teacher's Report Form,* which are 113-item measures of several factors of misbehavior: anxious/depressed, withdrawn/depressed, somatic complaints, social problems, thought problems, attention problems, rule-breaking behavior, and aggressive behavior (this scale also has an adolescent self-report version for 11–18-year-olds, the *Youth Self-Report*).
- *Conners Ratings Scales* (Parent and Teacher Versions-Revised), which are 80-item (long version) or 27-item (short version) measures of several factors of misbehavior: oppositional, cognitive problems/inattention, hyperactivity, anxious-shy, perfectionism, social problems, and psychosomatic (for long version).
- *Child Symptom Inventory-4* (Parent Checklist; 97 items and Teacher Checklist; 77 items), which screen for the following problems: attention deficit/hyperactivity disorder, oppositional defiant disorder, conduct disorder, generalized anxiety disorder, social phobia, separation anxiety disorder, obsessive-compulsive disorder, specific phobia, major depressive disorder, dysthymic disorder, schizophrenia, pervasive developmental disorder, and motor and vocal tics.

Information for obtaining these scales is presented in Appendix 2. Questionnaires have the advantage of providing substantial information about a child's behavior problems in a short period of time. However, questionnaires generally provide *global* information about a child's misbehavior and do not provide information necessarily specific to one child's school refusal behavior. For example, a questionnaire may inform you that a child generally withdraws from others. The questionnaire will not inform you, however, of specific social and performance situations at school a child may be avoiding. Thus, you should use questionnaires but combine information from these scales with specific information about a child's behavior with respect to school attendance.

Reviewing Records

Different schools keep different kinds of records, so the recommendations I make here are broad in nature. However, schools are notorious sometimes for their record-keeping, and you can use this to your advantage when assessing a youth with school refusal behavior. In particular, *reviewing attendance and academic records* is recommended. Academic records can give you important information about a child's grades and current status. This is especially important when considering a youth such as Luke, whose grades are suffering and who might fail the school year. An honest appraisal is needed of the probability a child will fail the school year and whether full-time attendance is futile or irrelevant. Many youths ask me, for example, why they should attend school from April to June when they have already failed the school year. This is a legitimate question to address if some attendance is to be realistically expected.

Knowing a child's academic status will help you determine a good course of action for the remainder of the school year. Can the child still salvage some credit? Can the child still pass the school year under some conditions, such as summer school? Can a 504 or other plan (see Chapter 5) be established so a child has hope of receiving some academic credit and an incentive for coming to school? Outlining a systemic, alternative educational plan for the late part of the school year is often a key element for addressing adolescents with school refusal behavior.

Attendance records are critically important as well. Some attendance records are better than others. Those with more detail, listing instances of tardiness and partial and complete absences, for example, will obviously be more useful. In addition to establishing a reliable baseline of absenteeism, attendance records are helpful when educating parents about the scope of a child's problem and for resolving contradictory reports about how much school a child has actually attended. If your school has an attendance officer, this person could be part of the intervention by informing you and the student's parents immediately of an unexcused absence by a particular child.

Formal Testing

Much of what has been described in this chapter falls under the rubric of behavioral assessment. Behavioral assessment methods measure the forms and functions of problems such as school refusal behavior by focusing on specific and daily conduct. Monitoring daily absenteeism, administering the SRAS-R or other questionnaires, asking questions about events at school, watching a child's temper tantrum on a playground, and reviewing school records are all examples of the specifics of behavioral assessment.

Many school-based social workers, school psychologists, and other personnel are particularly adept at administering more global assessments such as achievement and intelligence tests. Such *formal testing* can also include measures of personality, memory, or even general neuropsychological functioning or psychopathology. In general, a behavioral assessment approach is recommended for as fluid a behavior as problematic absenteeism. However, formal testing has its place as part of the assessment process for this population.

How so? First, formal testing can provide you with an excellent profile of a child's cognitive and academic abilities. As mentioned in Chapter 1, school refusal behavior is commonly associated with learning problems. A child struggling in school can obviously be poorly motivated to complete work or even come to class, so diagnosing and treating an existing learning disorder or related problem is important. More severe developmental disorders such as Asperger's disorder or autism can obviously interfere with school attendance as well and must be addressed.

Second, knowing a child's cognitive abilities will help you understand how much a child comprehends his absentee problem and whether you can use a cognitive approach (see Chapter 3). Younger children, those with developmental disorders, or youths with less developed cognitive abilities require a more concrete or behavioral approach to intervention. However, children with excellent cognitive abilities may respond well to thinking-based approaches covered in Chapter 3.

Third, formal testing can provide you with information about comorbid problems such as depression or attention-deficit/hyperactivity disorder. In some cases, these problems can be more severe than absenteeism and must be addressed first. A youth who is severely depressed and suicidal, for example, will not respond well to an intervention that focuses first on school attendance. Other youths who are extremely distressed or who have other severe behavior problems may require medication prior to discussions about resuming school attendance. Conferring with a clinical child psychologist or psychiatrist (see Chapter 1) is strongly recommended in these cases.

Putting the Assessment Information Together

We have covered many different ways to collect information about a child with school refusal behavior. Putting all of this information together, however, can be a bit of a challenge. Once you have conducted as thorough an assessment as possible, look for patterns of behavior among your data. For example, are parent reports and your observations of behavior consistent? In the case of Olivia, you may find that parent reports of severe distress and observed tantrums on the playground before school are indeed consistent. Or are SRAS-R ratings consistent with daily monitoring data? In the case of Luke, you may find that his skipping out after lunch is consistent with SRAS-R ratings of pursuit of tangible rewards outside of school.

As you search for patterns in your data, form an opinion about what maintains a child's school refusal behavior. Concentrate on the four functions of school refusal behavior described in this chapter and in Chapter 1. Consider the possibility as well, especially in more chronic cases, that a child is refusing school for more than one reason. As you form this opinion, talk again to parents, teachers, and knowledgeable others about your hypothesis and see if they agree.

You may find at this point that a child's school refusal picture is unclear. This may indicate that people cannot supply you with good information because they themselves are unsure what is happening. Or a child may be out of school for such a long time that school-based personnel cannot tell you anything. In other cases, parents disagree with one another, or parents and children disagree about the forms and function of school refusal behavior. In these cases, you will have to consider the preponderance of evidence in one direction or another. In addition, your own behavioral observations will become more critical in these kinds of cases.

Once you form a hypothesis as to why a child refuses school, you can confirm your belief by conducting mini-experiments. In Olivia's case, for example, you might allow her to sit in your office or the school library without penalty for a couple of days. If she attends without difficulty, then this supports your hypothesis that Olivia is refusing school to avoid classroom-based distress. In Luke's case, you might provide a large incentive for him to attend school completely for two days. If successful, then this confirms your belief that Luke's school attendance or nonattendance is based on tangible rewards. A child you suspect of refusing school for attention could be allowed to have a parent attend school with him for a day to see if attendance is suddenly nonproblematic. This must obviously be done with caution, however, because doing so temporarily rewards the child for misbehavior.

Once the assessment and confirmation process is as complete as possible, meet with a child's parents and fully explain your thinking. Provide specific examples of how a child's behavior is maintained over time. Olivia, for example, is sometimes brought home by her parents, which reinforces her anxious school refusal behavior. Luke spends time with his friends in the afternoon, which reinforces his absence from school. Encourage parents to challenge your findings, but provide as much evidence for your opinion as possible.

Finally, provide parents with a rationale for the intervention you decide to choose. If a child's school refusal behavior is anxiety based, such as Olivia's, then carefully point out how an anxiety management strategy might be helpful (see Chapter 3). If a child's school refusal behavior is tangibly reward based, such as Luke's, then carefully point out how increased supervision and negotiation of rewards for school attendance might be helpful (see Chapter 4). Ask parents to commit to the strategy you outline and fully answer their questions.

Final Comments and What's Next

Assessing a child's forms and function of school refusal behavior can be arduous but is extremely important. In fact, the assessment process should continue throughout your intervention and even beyond. Indeed, extensive monitoring of a child's daily attendance should remain intact indefinitely in cases of school refusal behavior because slips and relapse are common (see Chapter 6). This chapter provided you with a general framework and some tools for assessing youths with school refusal behavior. Focusing on the daily "nuts and bolts" of a child's behavior is critical.

The next two chapters discuss strategies for addressing youths with negatively reinforced and positively reinforced school refusal behavior. Chapter 3 talks about methods to reduce a child's distress about school and to gradually increase attendance. Chapter 4 describes methods of enhancing parent control and negotiating solutions to address youths who pursue rewards outside of school. A particular focus will be made on describing the procedures and how school officials can adopt and implement them within a school setting.

3

Interventions for Negatively Reinforced School Refusal Behavior

Kendra is an 8-year-old girl in third grade who has been having enormous difficulty entering school and remaining in class for an entire day. Kendra often sobs on the playground before school and cries softly in her classroom for most of the day if she does attend. She has already had several unexcused absences this year and her parents, though motivated to solve the problem, are frustrated and confused about what to do next. Kendra commonly complains of stomachaches and headaches at school and has asked repeatedly to be placed in home schooling.

David is a 13-year-old boy in eighth grade who has substantial difficulty attending all of his classes. Although David is a good student and usually attends school in the morning, he commonly skips classes that involve some performance before others. In particular, he skips all physical education classes and many of his math and reading classes. David is a shy child with few friends who often withdraws from others. He has been known to eat his lunch, for example, in the bathroom to avoid the cafeteria. David is now failing physical education and has begun receiving detentions for his absences.

You may recall from Chapter 1 that many kids refuse school for *negative reinforcement*. This means they refuse school to avoid or escape something aversive or upsetting related to the school setting. Youths who refuse school for negative reinforcement generally do so for one or both of the following reasons, or functions:

- To avoid school-related stimuli that provoke negative affectivity (combination of anxiety and depression) or general distress (like Kendra).

- To escape aversive social and/or evaluative situations at school (like David).

Recall that the first function generally involves younger children, and the second function generally involves older children and adolescents. Youths could refuse school for both reasons, however. Children who refuse school for the first function often cannot clearly identify what bothers them about school, though transitions from one part of the school setting to another are often problematic. Youths who refuse school for the second function, however, are usually able to tell you what specific social and performance situations at school they intensely dislike.

This chapter outlines strategies for addressing youths like Kendra and David who refuse school for negative reinforcement. Each clinical intervention procedure is described, along with ways they can be adopted for practice in an academic setting by school-based personnel. Because time constraints are more pressing in a school than a clinical setting, this chapter suggests modifications to the treatments to accommodate these constraints. As a clinician, I typically work more with the child than the parents in cases of school refusal for negative reinforcement. In a school setting, however, you will likely have to work with parents and the child together from the start to accelerate the intervention process.

For youths who refuse school for negative reinforcement, key intervention procedures include education about the nature of anxiety/distress, techniques to manage physical anxiety, modification of irrational cognitions (thoughts), and gradual reintroduction to the school setting. With the exception of the cognitive step, which is more appropriate for older children and adolescents, the procedures described in this chapter generally apply to all youths who refuse school for negative reinforcement. The sections that follow cover each of these intervention components.

Education about the Nature of Anxiety/Distress

If you are confronted with a child refusing school for negative reinforcement, like Kendra or David, then a good first step is to educate the child and parents about the nature of his or her anxiety/distress. Recall from Chapter 1 that anxiety or distress consists of three main components:

- A *physical component,* such as trembling, muscle tension, "butterflies" in the stomach, nausea, or other bodily symptoms.

- A *cognitive or thinking component,* such as irrational or unjustified beliefs that everyone dislikes the child or is judging her harshly when she performs in some way before others.
- A *behavioral component,* such as avoiding certain events, fleeing or escaping upsetting situations, crying, temper tantrums, or non-compliance.

Recall as well from Chapter 1 that each of these components usually progresses in a *certain sequence* for a child. A child may awaken, for example, to physical feelings of nausea and achiness that produce thoughts of disaster at school and a desire not to go to class. These thoughts may then lead to certain behaviors such as refusing to get out of bed or running away from the school campus in the morning. Of course, anxiety sequences for other children may be different (see Chapter 1 for a description and illustration of different sequences).

From your assessment, you should have a good idea about what specific anxiety sequence exists for a particular child. It can be helpful to use visuals to show a child and his parents what seems to be happening in their situation. An example regarding Kendra is illustrated in Figure 3.1. In her case, physical feelings of anxiety are painful to her and help trigger basic thoughts about not wanting to go to school. In the case of younger children, the verbal statements you solicit about school will likely be quite rudimentary. This is why cognitive interventions are not emphasized with these kids. However, Kendra's physical feelings and thoughts do lead to problematic behaviors such as excessive crying and refusal to enter the school building.

Another example is illustrated in Figure 3.2, this time for David. David is older, so his cognitive development is at a point when he can likely give you more detail about his thoughts. In David's case, his thoughts are the key anxiety component that begins his sequence toward school refusal behavior. His thoughts of disaster at school understandably trigger upsetting physical feelings of anguish and then avoidance of classes and others at school.

When discussing a particular anxiety sequence with a child and parents, use multiple, specific, and recent examples from the child's own experiences. Encourage the child and parents to disagree with you if their observations differ radically from yours. If necessary, collect additional information from family members to modify your view of the child's anxiety sequence. Most important, be sure all relevant family members

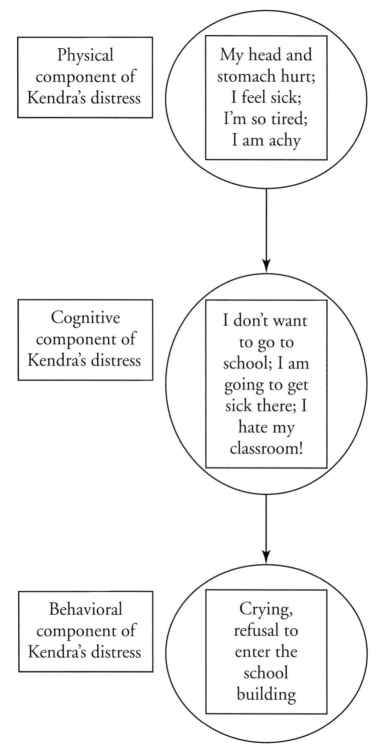

Figure 3.1.

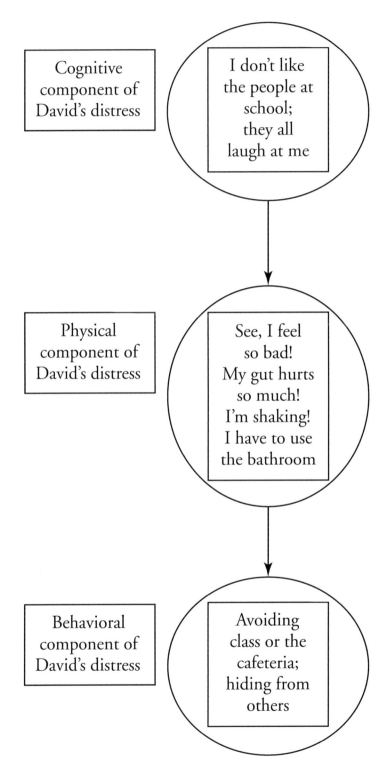

Figure 3.2.

fully understand the sequence you outlined because the sequence will serve as the rationale for the intervention you will propose. Specifically, you will recommend to the family that each component of the child's anxiety—physical, cognitive, and behavioral—must be addressed if the child is to resume full-time school attendance with less distress.

Modifications for a School Setting

Educating a student about the nature of anxiety/distress in a clinic setting does not have to differ much from educating a student in a school setting. However, as mentioned earlier, time constraints are likely an issue so you should meet with the child *and* parents together to outline what you think is happening in their situation. In addition, you may not have time to outline the anxiety sequence and then schedule another meeting with the family. Instead, you may have to accomplish as much as you can during this initial meeting. As such, use the sequence to convince family members to address each aspect of anxiety and encourage family members to commit to a plan of action. Components of this plan are discussed in the following sections.

It is important that you convey to family members the need to practice all interventions described in this chapter. The analogy I commonly give to children and parents is that managing anxiety involves learning a new skill. Ask the child to give you an example of some skill he has recently learned, such as riding a bicycle, skiing, or playing a song on the piano. Ask the child to describe the learning process, which surely required some adult help at the beginning as well as some pratfalls. With practice, however, the child was able to complete the skill more independently. The same is true for anxiety management—initially, going to school and managing upsetting feelings will be difficult. With practice, however, the skill will become much easier, and the child will find that attending school is a much more palatable option.

Managing Physical Feelings of Anxiety/Distress

Once a child and her parents understand the notion of physical, cognitive, and behavioral components of anxiety or distress, as well as her specific sequence of components, then progressing to the next step is desirable. For many youths, physical feelings of anxiety are particularly bothersome and often trigger the distress sequences illustrated here and in Chapter 1. Therefore, helping a child control her physical feelings of anxiety is important. Different methods of helping a child control physical feelings are available. The following sections describe methods that are most feasible, portable, and time efficient. Two methods in particular involve managing one's breathing and engaging in progressive muscle relaxation.

Breathing

A simple way to help a child reduce physical feelings of distress is to teach him to breathe correctly. Many children experience shortness of breath, breathe shallowly, or hyperventilate when upset. Doing so actually makes the feeling of anxiety worse, so helping a child regulate breathing is important. Have the child sit before you in a comfortable position. *Then ask the child to breathe in slowly through his nose (with mouth closed) and breathe out slowly through his mouth.* As the child does so, encourage him to breathe deeply into his diaphragm (between the abdomen and chest and just below the rib cage). The child may need to push two fingers into his diaphragm to experience the sensation of a full, deep breath. The child can then breathe slowly out of his mouth. Parents may even join the process to help their child practice at home.

For younger children such as Kendra, I recommend creating an image during the breathing technique. Kendra could imagine blowing up a tire or pretend she is a large, floating balloon. As Kendra breathes in, she can imagine filling up with fuel and energy. As she breathes out, she can imagine losing fuel or energy (or tension). The child must come to understand the difference between feeling tense when lungs are full of air and feeling more relaxed after breathing out. The following breathing script may be helpful (adapted from Kearney and Albano, 2007):

Pretend you are a hot air balloon. When you breathe in, you are filling the balloon with air so it can go anywhere you want. Breathe in through your nose like this (show for your child). Breathe slowly and deeply—try to breathe in a lot of air! Now breathe out slowly through your mouth like air leaving a balloon. Count slowly in your head as you breathe out . . . . 1 . . . . 2 . . . . 3 . . . . 4 . . . . 5. Let's try this again (practice at least 3 times).

Key advantages of the breathing method are its ease, brevity, and portability. The child can use this method in different stressful situations and usually without drawing the attention of others. I recommend a child practice this breathing method at least three times per day for a few minutes at a time. In addition, the child should practice in the morning before school and during particularly stressful times at school. Some kids benefit as well by practicing this technique in the evening before school, especially Sunday evenings.

Muscle Relaxation

Another method of helping a child reduce physical feelings of anxiety is progressive muscle relaxation. Youths such as Kendra or David are usually quite tense in different areas of their body, especially in the shoulders, face, and stomach. Different methods of muscle relaxation are available, but a preferred one is a *tension-release method* in which a child physically tenses, holds, and then releases a specific muscle group. For example, a child may ball his hand into a fist, squeeze as tightly as possible and hold the tension for 10 seconds, and then suddenly release the grip (try it). When this is done two or three times in a row, people generally report feelings of warmth in the muscle as well as relaxation.

Muscle relaxation via tension-release can be done in different ways. When I work with children, I use a relaxation script that covers most areas of the body. I first ask the child to sit in a comfortable position and close her eyes. I then read the script slowly and ask the child to participate. You may wish to use the following script with a child (adapted from Ollendick and Cerny, 1981):

(Speaking slowly and in a low voice) Okay, sit down, try to relax, and close your eyes. Try to make your body droopy and floppy, like you are a wet towel. Take your right hand and squeeze it as hard as you can. Hold it tight! (Wait 5–10 seconds.) Now let go quickly. Good job. Let's do that again. Take your right hand and squeeze it as hard as you can. Hold it. (Wait 5–10 seconds.) Now let go quickly. See how that feels. Nice and warm and loose. Now take your left hand and squeeze it as hard as you can. Hold it tight! (Wait 5–10 seconds.) Now let go quickly. Good job. Let's do that again. Take your left hand and squeeze it as hard as you can. Hold it. (Wait 5–10 seconds.) Now let go quickly. See how that feels. Nice and warm and loose.

Now shrug your shoulders hard and push them up to your ears. Make your shoulders really tight. Hold them there. (Wait 5–10 seconds.) Now let go quickly. Great. Let's do that again. Shrug your shoulders hard and push them up to your ears. Make your shoulders really tight. Hold them there. (Wait 5–10 seconds.) Now let go quickly. Great job.

Now scrunch up your face as much as you can. Make your face seem really small and tight. Now hold it there. (Wait 5–10 seconds.) Now let your face go droopy. Good. Let's do that again. Scrunch up your face as much as you can. Make your face seem really small and tight. Now hold it there. (Wait 5–10 seconds.) Now let your face go droopy. Good job.

Now I want you to bite down real hard with your teeth. Make your jaw really tight. Hold it there. (Wait 5–10 seconds.) Now open your jaw. How does that feel? Good. Let's try that again. Bite down real hard with your teeth. Make your jaw really tight. Hold it there. (Wait 5–10 seconds.) Now open your jaw. Try to make it as loose as you can. Good practicing!

Let's go to your stomach now. Bring in your stomach as much as you can—make it real tight! Press it against your backbone. Now hold it there. (Wait 5–10 seconds.) Now let go quickly. That feels better. Let's try that again. Bring in your stomach as much as you can—make it real tight! Press it against your backbone. Now hold it there. (Wait 5–10 seconds.) Now let go quickly. Great job.

Okay, one more. Push your feet onto the floor real hard so your legs feel really tight. Push hard! Now hold it. (Wait 5–10 seconds.) Now relax your legs. Shake them a little. Let's try that again. Push your feet onto the floor real hard so your legs feel really tight. Push hard! Now hold it. (Wait 5–10 seconds.) Now relax your legs. Shake them a little. Good practicing!

Now try to make your whole body really droopy—pretend you are a wet towel! Relax your whole body and see how nice that feels. You did a great job relaxing. Okay, open your eyes.

You may wish to audiotape this script so a child can play it back when practicing. Encourage the child to practice this script at least twice per day in the beginning of your intervention and then once or twice per day as she becomes more adept and independent. In addition, the child could practice the method during times of the day when she feels most distressed. In Kendra's case, for example, she could practice relaxation with her mother on the playground immediately before school. In David's case, he could practice relaxation immediately before some social or performance situation at school.

Modifications for a School Setting

Because of time constraints, you may wish to teach a child relaxation techniques immediately after educating family members about anxiety. In addition, you may wish to teach breathing and muscle relaxation at one time so a child can use one or both right away. Some kids prefer one approach over the other, which is fine. The important thing is that a child practice and use the techniques as soon as possible.

In situations when time is highly constrained, using breathing and *partial* muscle relaxation may be preferred. In partial muscle relaxation, you or a child chooses one or two areas of the child's body that are particularly tense and the child practices the tension-release method *only on those areas.* In David's case, for example, he may say his shoulders and stomach are tensest when at school. To save time, therefore, you could concentrate your efforts on these two areas only.

If you cannot meet with a family, then recommending commercially available breathing and relaxation tapes might be an option. The child might even download relaxation mp3s to his iPod or other mp3 player. In addition, you could help a child practice relaxation techniques during times you know he is particularly distressed at school. Helping a child relax in your office immediately before physical education class, for example, might be feasible. You may also need to solicit the help of teachers who can take an anxious child aside and help her practice relaxing.

Cognitive Procedures

So far this chapter has talked about ways of managing the physical aspects of a child's anxiety. Another key component of anxiety in this population is *irrational cognitions or thoughts* related to the school setting. This is especially so for older children and adolescents with more advanced cognitive development who worry about aversive social and/ or evaluative situations. In David's case, for example, he commonly worried about performing so badly in front of people that everyone would laugh at him. Youths in this group commonly worry about catastrophic things or the "worst-case scenario" happening to them, usually deep embarrassment, humiliation, or exclusion from others after some public performance (see Chapter 1 for specific examples).

In my practice with these youths, I try to move them toward more rational and realistic thinking in different social and performance situations. Notice that I did not say more positive thinking, but rather more *realistic* thinking. Arbitrarily replacing negative thoughts with positive thoughts will not work and can actually make a situation worse. A child intensely anxious about taking tests, for example, will not benefit from "happy" thoughts or statements such as "Don't worry" once the test arrives. Instead, the same worries *will occur* and a child will grow even more concerned because thinking positive thoughts does not seem to be working. What we want to do, therefore, is help a child understand that difficult events *will* happen in life, but how he perceives and manages these events helps determine his anxiety level.

Identifying Types of Negative Thoughts

How can we help a youth think more realistically? The first thing to do is teach a youth and his parents about different kinds of negative thoughts or mental errors kids commonly make in social and performance situations. Following are the most common examples:

- Assuming something terrible is happening when actually it is not. David, for example, may assume people are laughing at him as he eats lunch when they are really just laughing at a joke.
- Assuming terrible things will happen when actually terrible things are not likely to happen. A teenager might assume others will bully him at school even though this has never happened and is not very likely to happen.
- Assuming what others are thinking when really one cannot know. This is called *mind reading* and can occur when a youth walks down a hallway wrongly assuming everyone believes her to be ugly.
- Assuming the consequences of one's actions will be terrible. This is called *jumping to conclusions* or "making mountains out of mole-hills" and can occur when a youth assumes handing in a math worksheet with a couple of mistakes on it will necessarily lead to a failing grade for that semester.
- Assuming one will be embarrassed and that embarrassment will linger and be excruciating. In David's case, for example, he assumed his performance in physical education would be so awful he would be humiliated and shamed for weeks.
- Assuming situations must be perfect or terrible with no intermediate "gray" areas. Youths often see situations in black and white, as when a teenager focuses on one bad event in his day and downplays all of the good things that happened.
- Assuming one must focus more on the negative than the positive in a situation. Anxious youths commonly focus more on the negative

aspect of a situation, as when a child focuses only on one kid snickering during his presentation instead of everyone else paying attention appropriately.

- Assuming blame for things not within their control. Adolescents, who are naturally egocentric anyway, sometimes go too far and blame themselves for things that have little to do with them, such as parents fighting or a classmate failing a test.

Discuss each of these problematic thoughts at length with a child and parents and determine which seem most pertinent. You may be able to draw some examples from your assessment when doing so. It may be helpful to design a list from these bullet points and give it to the child for constant referral. The child should become able to quickly identify errors in thinking. A child who walks into a classroom and immediately assumes some kids are snickering at her could stop, think about what kind of assumption she just made (bullet point #1 in this case), and design a more realistic thought (to be discussed).

A potential problem when trying to get specific thoughts from teenagers is they commonly say "I don't know" when you ask about a given situation. Or they give you snippets of a thought that are not very helpful. In these situations, ask a child to keep a written diary of thoughts when in a particularly stressful situation. David, for example, could be asked to write down his thoughts when eating lunch in the cafeteria or in the 5-minute period before an oral presentation. If a child is still unable to produce extensive thoughts, then ask him to perform some anxiety-provoking task before you, such as reading a newspaper article, and periodically ask him to say what he is thinking. Keep in mind that some kids are simply not very good at producing their thoughts, so emphasizing other techniques in this chapter might be a good idea in these cases.

Developing More Realistic Thoughts

Once a child understands what kinds of irrational thoughts exist and has a good handle on what kinds of mental errors she is making, the next step is to engage in more realistic thinking. This is done when other people and preferably the child himself challenges a negative thought and develops a more realistic one. Because you are not likely to have much time to do this, you may present the child (and parents) with a basic model that relies on the acronym *STOP* (adapted from Silverman and Kurtines, 1996):

- **S:** Am I **S**cared or nervous about a certain social or performance situation?
- **T:** What **T**houghts am I having in this situation?
- **O:** What **O**ther, more realistic thoughts can I have?
- **P: P**raise myself for thinking more realistic thoughts.

In this model, a child must first identify whether he is truly anxious in a given situation (the "S" component). Most adolescents know exactly what social and performance situations at school upset them the most, so this should not be a problem. If it is a problem, go back to your assessment and point out specific situations that seem difficult for the child. You may wish to rely on just four to five situations that are most problematic. The child should also inform you of any new social and performance situations that become stressful for him as school attendance increases.

Once a child knows she is in a stressful social or performance situation, she should engage in the second component of the stop model ("T"). She should identify what thoughts occur to her first in that situation. Hannah may enter a gymnasium during physical education class, for example, and immediately assume everyone is looking at her misshapen body in her uniform. The "T" component should be fairly easy to do because you have already educated her about the different cognitive mistakes kids make in these situations. In addition, you have already noted cognitive mistakes that are specific to Hannah.

The crucial part of this process is the next step ("O"). *The child must create an alternative, more realistic thought about what is happening in the situation.* In Hannah's case, for example, she should test her belief by observing what people are doing in the gymnasium. She will likely see that people are milling about, waiting for the physical education teacher, or talking among themselves. Hannah can see that, even if one or two people happen to look at her, the entire class is not doing so. In addition, she has no idea what people are thinking as she enters class. In this case, Hannah has closely evaluated the situation and arrived at a more realistic thought: people are not generally looking at me and those who are could be thinking about many different things and not me.

If a child successfully develops an alternative, more realistic thought, she should praise herself for doing so ("P"). Hannah could give herself a literal or figurative pat on the back for correcting an irrational belief. The STOP cycle is one that a child like David or Hannah must practice on a continual basis. Developing alternative, healthy, realistic thoughts must become a regularly practiced skill to avoid falling back into old assumptions about worst-case scenarios.

Assisting the Development of More Realistic Thoughts

A first thing you can do to help a child develop more realistic thoughts is reassure him that his thoughts, even if negative and skewed, are normal and universal. Everyone has negative and irrational thoughts, but a key difference between anxious and nonanxious people is that the latter can balance negative thoughts with more realistic thinking. A second thing you can do is provide the child with an index card of questions he can ask himself when confronted with a difficult thought. These questions are called *dispute handles* because a child uses the questions to challenge or dispute a negative or unrealistic thought (adapted from Kearney and Albano, 2007):

- Am I 100% sure this will happen (or is happening)?
- Can I really know what that person thinks of me?
- What's the worst thing that can really happen?
- Have I ever been in this situation before and was it really that bad?
- How many times has this terrible thing actually happened?
- Am I the only person that has ever had to deal with this situation?
- So what if I am not perfect in this situation?
- Is this really my fault?

A third thing you can do to assist the STOP process is provide a child with a simple worksheet to keep track of the STOP steps in a given situation. A sample worksheet is provided here (see Worksheet 3.1). You can distribute it to a child so she can log the STOP steps in a stressful situation. In Hannah's case, for example, she could write down in the "S" column "walking into gym class." The "T" column could be filled with different problematic thoughts such as "Everyone is staring at me" and "They all think I'm fat and ugly." The "O" column should contain more realistic thoughts such as "Only a couple of people are looking my way" and "I can't read people's minds and know what they are thinking." The "P" column could include self-verbalizations such as "Good job!" or "I am proud of myself for thinking differently."

Worksheet 3.1

Situations at school that bother me ("S")	My thoughts in this situation ("T")	Other, helpful thoughts I can have ("O")	Praise myself ("P")

A fourth thing you can do to assist the STOP process is role play with a child how to engage in STOP for a given situation. Let's return to Hannah's situation, for example, and her assumption that others are staring at her and judging her body in a negative way. You might have the following conversation with her:

You:	Okay, you've said that walking into gym class is really hard for you to do, that's a big "S" for you. One thought you had in the "T" column was that everyone would be staring at you. Is that right?
Hannah:	Yeah, I walk in and everybody looks around. I feel so embarrassed.
You:	I know it's hard sometimes to walk into gym class. Let's talk about the "O" part a little bit, maybe some other thoughts you could have in that situation. Are you 100% sure everyone is looking at you? Be honest.
Hannah:	No, I guess not 100%. I don't know.
You:	Okay, good, so you're not sure. What else might be going on?
Hannah:	Well, everybody's standing around, waiting for class to start. Everybody looks a little bored.
You:	What are they doing?
Hannah:	I don't know, talking to each other, hanging out on the bleachers.
You:	Are they all staring at you?
Hannah:	No, I guess not. Maybe just a couple of people.
You:	Okay, good, so an "Other" thought might be that just a couple of people are looking my way and not everybody, is that accurate?
Hannah:	Yeah, that's right. I guess it's not everybody.
You:	Great. A second thought in your "T" column was that everyone was thinking you are fat and ugly.
Hannah:	Yeah, I hate that gym uniform and how it looks.
You:	Yes, those uniforms are kind of unusual. Everyone has to wear one, right?
Hannah:	Yeah, they look pretty bad on everybody.
You:	So you're not the only one that looks different in her uniform.

HANNAH: Yeah, that's true, even the pretty girls look kinda weird.

YOU: Can you really know what other people are thinking of you?

HANNAH: No, I guess not. They can't know what I'm thinking either I guess.

YOU: Right! Good job. So what might be an "Other" thought?

HANNAH: That I don't know what people are thinking, it could be good or bad.

YOU: Right, great job again!

In this situation, you see the person Hannah was talking to used a couple of dispute handles to help her student arrive at more realistic thoughts (for examples of other role-play conversations, see "step one" in this series). The student must practice this process over time. In the beginning, Hannah could rely on a school counselor to help her with the STOP process. Over time, however, she should be able to apply it independently.

The last thing you can do to facilitate the STOP process is emphasize to youths that *embarrassment is a universal, temporary, and manageable condition.* Youths who dread social and performance situations nearly always worry most about becoming embarrassed or humiliated in some way (the worst-case scenario). Convey to a youth that embarrassment is something everyone feels from time to time (you may wish to share an embarrassing story of your own). In addition, embarrassment is a feeling that does not linger for days or weeks on end but usually dissipates quickly. Finally, show the child he was able to handle or manage past episodes of embarrassment and teach him ways of doing so in the future. We often handle embarrassment by laughing at ourselves, remembering that everyone experiences embarrassment at some time in his life, and knowing that the unpleasant feeling does not last long and will eventually decline.

Finally, you may wish to set up little experiments that will let a child test her erroneous beliefs. A student may claim, for example, that a classmate will hang up on her if she calls to ask about a homework assignment. In this case, you can ask the student about the probability of this actually happening. Anxious students usually overestimate the chance of disaster, so this student might say "70%." You could then give her your estimate (10%) and ask her to test her "hypothesis."

When the student comes back to you to report what happened, and says she and the classmate had a good conversation, remind her that she overestimated the chance of her classmate hanging up on her. Try as well to get anxious students to avoid "all-or-none" language such as "I can't do this" or "It will always be this way." Focus on words that allow for more flexibility about events, such as "sometimes" and "maybe."

Modifications for a School Setting

Cognitive procedures work well, but you may not have the time or resources for constant role plays. If you are working with a youth in these kinds of procedures, try to meet with her briefly at least once a day, perhaps in the morning, to cover potential obstacles that day and how she can best address difficult situations. In addition, encourage parents as much as possible to assume this role by having regular conversations with their child in the morning before school or in the evening about sensitive social and performance situations and how alternative thoughts can be developed.

Note as well that the cognitive procedures described here will not be effective for youths with negative thoughts that *are* realistic. A teenager may worry excessively about being bullied in a school hallway. If this circumstance is likely, then asking the child to think about the situation differently is pointless and even counterproductive. Instead, you must address the realistic threat *before* engaging in the procedures described here. However, cognitive procedures may apply in situations when a specific threat has been permanently removed and yet a child still worries excessively about physical harm, negative evaluation from others, or embarrassment.

Keep in mind as well that cognitive skills are not a substitute for social skills. If a child is truly unskilled when speaking to others or performing before others, then she must develop and practice social skills. You may have a social skills training group at your school that you can refer a child to, or you may ask parents to seek counseling for their child to learn these skills. Cognitive procedures will work best for youths with the basic knowledge needed to speak to others effectively and make friends. Cognitive procedures can precede or accompany methods to address the most important component of youths who refuse school for negative reinforcement: the behavioral component.

Gradual Reintroduction to the School Setting

To this point, this chapter has covered ways of addressing physical and cognitive components of anxiety among youths refusing school for negative reinforcement. The most important procedure in this chapter, however, involves addressing the behavioral component of anxiety. The behavioral component of anxiety is typically manifested most by *avoidance* of school-related situations, as in Kendra's case, or by *escape* from aversive school-related social and/or evaluative situations, as in David's case.

For those kids missing a great deal of school, we must establish a schedule whereby a child gradually attends more and more school or class time over a period of days or weeks. For those kids already attending school but with great difficulty, we must establish a schedule for reducing their distress in key situations such as attending physical education class or taking tests. This section is therefore divided into each type of case.

For Those Kids Missing Much School

If a child is missing substantial amounts of school time and you have worked with the family to address her physical and perhaps cognitive components of anxiety, then the next step is to establish a schedule whereby she gradually but increasingly attends school. As a child does so, be sure to continue to work on breathing, muscle relaxation, and changing irrational thoughts to help her manage key symptoms of anxiety. Also, be sure to fully discuss with the child and parents what kind of reintegration schedule they and you would like to pursue. *You, the child, and the parents must be on the same page with respect to the pace and scope of the reintegration process.* This section largely refers to kids who are completely out of school. If a child is attending school for at least part of the day, then the reintegration process could be based on the steps described here and accelerated.

If a child has been out of school and you and the parents feel he is now ready to resume regular classroom or school attendance, then consider the following ways of doing so:

- Have the child enter school and class in the morning and stay for a limited time, such as an hour, before being allowed to go home. The child is then expected to gradually increase his amount of school time, such as an extra hour every three days, until full-time attendance is reached (e.g., staying until 10:00 A.M., then 11:00 A.M., then noon and working forward).

- Let the child enter school near the end of the school day, such as 2:00 P.M., before coming home when school normally ends (e.g., 3:10 P.M.). The child is then expected to gradually increase her amount of school time, such as an extra hour every three days, until full-time attendance is reached (e.g., arriving at 1:00 P.M., then noon, then 11:00 A.M. and working backward).
- Let the child attend school only for lunch initially before being allowed to come home. He is then expected to gradually increase his amount of school time immediately before and after lunch, adding time from the middle and working outward. If lunch was scheduled at 12:00–12:30 P.M., for example, then the child might be expected next to attend school from 11:30 A.M. to 1:00 P.M.
- Have the child attend school only for her favorite class initially before being allowed to come home. In this scenario, a child picks a favorite class or time of day, such as science, and attends that section of the day only. The next favorite class or time of day is then added, followed by the third favorite class or time of day, and so forth.
- Have the child attend school in a setting other than the classroom initially. In this scenario, he attends some alternative school-based setting such as a counselor's office or library during the day. Once this is accomplished, the child begins to spend an increasing amount of time in the classroom.

Which method is best? The answer to this question depends on a particular child, though less risky methods are the first and last options. Both options require a child to enter the school building *in the morning,* which is beneficial for two reasons. First, a child will have to continue to practice morning preparation behaviors even if he is to attend school only from 8:50 to 9:50 A.M. In the other scenarios, a child could delay getting ready for school, or sleep in, which will eventually have to change. Parents will find it easier if they can avoid working on school attendance *and* morning preparation behaviors at the same time.

A second reason the morning scenarios are preferred is that even if a child initially balks at attending, there is still time to try to get her into school for at least part of the day. If parents cannot get a child to attend school at the regularly scheduled time of 8:50 A.M., for example, they may still be able to get her there by 10:00 A.M. or noon or even 1:30 P.M. A downside of the afternoon approach (bullet point

#2) is that if a child balks at school attendance at 2:00 P.M., little time is left to salvage the day. This "dessert first" approach allows a child to stay home most of the day before school attendance is expected. I therefore recommend using the afternoon approach only with great caution and only if you are fully confident parents will bring their child to school at that time.

From the beginning of your reintegration plan, always expect a child to attend school at whatever minimum level he can accomplish or has accomplished. Recall from Chapter 2 that a key piece of information from the assessment is how far a child can approach and attend school. *This should be the minimum you and parents expect a child to do.* If a child, for example, can get ready for school in the morning and can sit in the school's main lobby for the day, this is the minimum behavior to be expected. You will find it much easier to reintegrate a child into a regular classroom setting if she already prepares for school in the morning and can withstand being physically in the school building. In other cases, I have asked parents to remain in the car with their child in the school parking lot until the child can enter the school building.

If a child is home during school hours, either before or after school attendance is expected, then he should complete academic work. Work sent home by teachers, reading and writing projects, worksheets, and other educational tasks should be emphasized. *The child should not be allowed fun activities during school hours.* In addition, should a child fail to meet the expected timeline for attendance, such as two hours in the morning, parents should issue punishments for this behavior (see Chapter 4). Rewards can be given after school hours for appropriate school attendance.

Parents often ask at this stage under what conditions can they keep a child home from school. I recommend downplaying most physical complaints such as stomachaches and headaches, particularly if a pediatrician has ruled out physical causes. *Convey to parents that the default option in the morning should always be to send the child to school, even if minor maladies exist.* Children may be kept home from school if one or more of the following conditions are present:

- A temperature of at least 100 degrees
- Frequent vomiting
- Bleeding
- Lice
- Severe diarrhea

- Severe flu-like symptoms
- Another very severe medical condition such as intense pain

As the child reintegrates into a regular classroom setting, anticipate problems that may suddenly occur. The child may show new behaviors to induce nonattendance, such as intense physical complaints, temper tantrums, disruptive behavior in the classroom, or constant visits to your office or the nurse's office. In these cases, a school's default policy is often to send the child home. *I strongly discourage sending home a child with a history of school refusal behavior following such problems.* Sending a child home only reinforces school refusal behavior and will make future intervention much more difficult. If a child is so disruptive he cannot stay in class, then options such as in-school suspension or detention are preferred to sending the child home.

For Those Kids Missing Less School

Other kids, such as David, may attend school fairly regularly but have great difficulty attending certain classes due to anxiety. Examples include youths who miss tests, eat lunch somewhere besides the cafeteria, or skip certain classes during the day that require social or evaluative performance. For these kids, a reintegration schedule is also needed but may be somewhat different in scope than the schedule used for kids missing most of school.

For those kids missing less school, we must first identify what aspects of school are missed the most. You should be able to draw from your assessment what kinds of situations are most problematic for a certain child. In David's case, for example, he was missing all of his physical education classes and many of his math and reading classes. He was also eating his lunch in the bathroom to avoid social interactions in the school cafeteria. In a case like David's, we first want to know all of these problems and then rank order the problems from least to most difficult, or anxiety provoking.

To do so, use the worksheet provided here (see Worksheet 3.2). You and the child, with parental input as necessary, can list 5–10 avoided or otherwise problematic situations that range from least to most anxiety provoking. In addition, each problematic item should be linked to two ratings on a 0–10 scale. The first rating is how anxious the child feels in the situation. The second rating is how much the child avoids or wishes to avoid the situation. Both ratings will likely be similar for each item, though not necessarily so. Some children do endure some situations with great dread but never avoid them or wish to avoid them.

Worksheet 3.2

Situations or Places That Scare Me!	Anxiety Rating	Avoidance Rating
1.		
2.		
3.		
4.		
5.		
6.		
7.		
8.		
9.		
10.		

```
X——X——X——X——X——X——X——X——X——X——X
0    1    2    3    4    5    6    7    8    9    10
None    A little    Some    Stronger    A lot    The worst
```

In David's case, the following hierarchy was developed:

Situations or Places That Scare Me	Anxiety Rating	Avoidance Rating
1. Attending and participating in physical education class	9	9
2. Giving an oral presentation in reading class	8	7
3. Writing on the blackboard in math class	6	6
4. Answering a question from a teacher in class	5	5
5. Eating lunch in the cafeteria	4	5

Addressing the behavioral component for someone like David means practicing these situations while engaging in appropriate relaxation and cognitive strategies to manage anxiety. Initially, this practice can be done at home or in your office. A child could, for example, practice oral presentations or answer questions in a relatively safe environment as you or parents provide feedback on his performance. In David's case, his parents could take him to public places to eat, ask him questions about his homework that he would have to answer before others, and have him read a newspaper article or book report to them. As the child relaxes physically, develops healthy thoughts, and practices difficult situations, he should become proficient in areas he struggles with at school.

Once a child becomes proficient at items on her hierarchy outside of school or in your office, then she must practice in real-life school situations. The best way to do so is to practice one step on the hierarchy at a time and begin with the lowest-rated item. In David's case, for example, he was initially asked to eat lunch in the school cafeteria but near the exit. Following several days of practice, he saw that terrible things were not happening to him and so he was asked to eat his lunch closer to the center of the cafeteria. This practice was continued until David's self-reported anxiety level was near zero. He was also asked to engage in social interactions with others as he ate lunch.

Once a child has mastered one step of the hierarchy, he then progresses to the next step. After consulting with David's teachers, the school counselor gave David several questions in advance that could be asked of him in class. He was initially allowed to prepare these answers and then answer them effectively in class. Doing so significantly reduced his anxiety and avoidance level, but he understood that the next step involved preparing and studying on his own to answer questions not given to him in advance. Later practices included writing on the blackboard in math class and giving oral presentations. These practices were initially done alone and then before classmates.

Advancing to the final rung of a child's anxiety/avoidance hierarchy is, of course, the most difficult aspect of this intervention. David had enormous difficulty attending physical education class, so this step was divided into several smaller ones. Specific concerns on David's part included dressing in the locker room, being picked last for a team, and performing poorly in a sport. David was initially allowed to dress in a segregated area of the locker room and, once comfortable with that, was gradually expected to dress more in the locker room. In consultation with David's physical education teacher, teams were drawn randomly from a hat for some time before the normal method of choosing was resumed. David was allowed to choose a team in some classes as well. Finally, the school counselor worked with David to reduce his concern about not performing so well in physical education class, focusing on the fact that others also did not always play well and that David was better at some sports than others. David's parents also took a more active role in helping David practice different sports at home.

Modifications for a School Setting

Reintegrating a child to a regular classroom setting can be prickly in time-limited situations. You may find that anxiety management techniques such as relaxation and changing negative thoughts have to be done concurrently with a reintegration schedule and not before. In other words, the child may have to practice managing all three components of anxiety at once. If this is the case, use a step-by-step process. Trying to force a child into school all at once is usually not productive.

In other cases, you simply do not have the time or resources to conduct many of the anxiety management techniques. Or, parents are not cooperative or enthusiastic about the relaxation or cognitive methods presented in this chapter. In this situation, I recommend addressing the behavioral component by gradually reintegrating a child into school or practicing difficult situations. As the child has some success with these, he may respond well to relaxation or cognitive methods afterward.

Try also to avoid common mistakes during this process. Some school officials become overly stern or "helpful" when they see a child on a part-time attendance schedule and then require him to attend more that day. If everyone has committed to the student attending for only two hours that day, and this is what the child expects, then suddenly requiring her to attend more class time will upset her and delay treatment success. On the other hand, in many cases children will spontaneously attend more school than their schedule calls for, and this should be allowed.

Another common mistake is to assume that a child who is finally in a given situation at school no longer has anxiety about being there. Obtaining anxiety ratings and reducing distress in these situations is key to preventing future relapse (see also Chapter 6). Finally, try to arrange circumstances at school so a child is not penalized for partial absences during reintegration. A child and his parents will be more motivated to help resume full-time school attendance if they know school officials support a gradual reintegration process emotionally and bureaucratically.

Final Comments and What's Next

This chapter covered strategies for addressing youths who refuse school for negative reinforcement or anxiety-based concerns. Be sure to tailor your intervention to the skills and cognitive development of a particular youth. Younger children, for example, usually cannot handle advanced cognitive techniques. In addition, older children and adolescents may not want to practice anxiety management techniques that draw attention to themselves.

Chapter 4 discusses methods of addressing youths who refuse school for positive reinforcement. This includes younger children who often refuse school for attention from significant others as well as older children and adolescents who often refuse school to pursue tangible rewards outside of school. Chapter 5 addresses difficult parents as well as other special topics and circumstances that often surround youths who refuse school for negative or positive reinforcement.

4

Interventions for Positively Reinforced School Refusal Behavior

Eevie is a 7-year-old girl who often refuses school because she wants to stay home with a parent. She commonly screams on the playground before school, wrapping herself tightly around her mother's legs or running back to the car. Eevie does attend class if a parent is in the school building, so Eevie's mother has taken a leave of absence from work to serve as a parent volunteer at her daughter's elementary school. Eevie also insists that her mother eat lunch with her in the school cafeteria and that her mother be at her classroom at exactly 3:15 P.M. to take her home. Eevie also commonly refuses to attend play dates or birthday parties if one of her parents cannot be there.

Alexander is a 16-year-old boy in eleventh grade who has been repeatedly skipping classes and leaving school grounds after lunch. Alexander often comes to school in the morning but meets friends in the morning who encourage him to miss school and engage in fun activities off-campus. He has 12 marked absences from school, but his guidance counselor believes the number is higher because Alexander is not always caught. His parents were recently informed of Alexander's absenteeism and are distraught. Alexander's grades are declining. In fact, he is in danger of failing the academic year.

Recall from Chapter 1 that many kids refuse school for *positive reinforcement*. This means they refuse school to pursue something alluring outside the school setting. Many of these youths are not particularly upset with anything related to school, though they could be. Instead, youths who refuse school for positive reinforcement generally do so for one of the following reasons, or functions:

- To pursue attention from significant others, such as a parent (like Eevie).
- To pursue tangible rewards outside of school (like Alexander).

Recall that the first function generally involves younger children and the second function generally involves older children and adolescents. Youths could also refuse school for one of these reasons in addition to functions of negative reinforcement discussed in Chapter 3. Children who refuse school for attention from significant others often insist on being with a parent much of the time. Although this seems to overlap with the construct of separation anxiety, youths who refuse school for attention are often manipulative, controlling, oppositional, and willful.

Youths who refuse school for specific tangible rewards outside of school often mingle with friends, visit public places, or enjoy the amenities of staying home. These youths keep their absenteeism as secret as possible and are often combative with parents and school officials to maintain the status quo. Some of these youths drift into other delinquent activities such as stealing, drug use, vandalism, and curfew breaking. In most cases, however, absenteeism from school is a primary problem.

This chapter outlines strategies for addressing youths like Eevie and Alexander who refuse school for positive reinforcement. As in Chapter 3, each intervention procedure is described and information on adapting these clinical procedures for practice in an academic setting by school-based personnel is provided. Again, because time constraints are more pressing in a school than a clinical setting, this chapter suggests modifications to the treatments to accommodate these constraints. As a clinician, I typically spend much time developing appropriate parental commands and developing written contracts for children who refuse school for positive reinforcement. You will likely not have the luxury of time to fully complete all the steps required of these techniques, so an abridged version of these procedures is presented for use in educational settings.

For youths who refuse school for attention, key intervention procedures focus on *parents* and include instituting a regular morning routine, attending to appropriate behaviors and ignoring inappropriate behaviors, establishing formal rewards and punishments for school attendance/nonattendance, altering parent commands, addressing excessive reassurance-seeking and clingy behavior, and forcing school attendance under certain circumstances. For youths who pursue tangible rewards outside of school, key intervention procedures focus on the *adolescent and parents* and include increasing supervision, developing written contracts to boost incentives for school attendance, escorting a child from class to class, and teaching a child to refuse offers to miss school.

Youths Refusing School for Attention

Unlike Chapter 3, where anxiety management procedures largely applied to both negative reinforcement functions, interventions are quite different for youths who refuse school for attention and youths who pursue tangible rewards outside of school. This chapter is therefore split between these two functions. For younger youths who refuse school for attention, like Eevie, much of your focus will be on the child's parents. The general goal of intervention is to increase parents' ability to attend to and reward a child's appropriate school attendance behaviors and downplay, ignore, or even formally punish school refusal behaviors. In addition, many parents require help establishing clear, structured morning routines. *The foundation of intervention for this function is to reestablish parent control.* A rationale for parents regarding this foundation is next.

Providing a Rationale for Intervention

Family members of children who refuse school for attention are often on "pins and needles" as they await what misbehavior a child will show in the morning. Many parents of these children, such as Eevie's parents, hold their breath, hope for the best, and bargain with their child to try to get her to school. Many of these kids have successfully learned the best time and place to resist going to school, often just as a family is about to leave the house, just as the car pulls up to the school playground, or just as the bell rings for school to start. Children who refuse school for attention often resist school at these vulnerable times, especially if a parent is late for work, because they know they can more easily induce parental acquiescence. As a result, parents find themselves "dancing to their child's tune" and doing what they can, including bribery and promises, to get their child to enter school. This must change. The goal of intervention, and the rationale you can provide to parents, is that *parents must reestablish control.*

One way to convey this to parents is by illustration. Figure 4.1 is a schematic that describes one child's attention-based school refusal behaviors and how parents may inappropriately respond to these behaviors and thus reinforce them. In contrast, the goal is to reestablish parental control through routines, rules, commands, rewards, and punishments so a child appropriately responds to parent directives (see Figure 4.2). Help parents see the dynamic that happens in the morning and get them to commit to a pattern of change toward greater parental control. One of the first methods for reestablishing parental control is instituting a set morning routine.

Instituting a Set Morning Routine

The most important aspect of intervention for youths who refuse school for attention, the intervention component from which other components will flow, is *instituting a set morning routine.* This involves working with parents to design a morning routine that is regular and predictable yet flexible enough to absorb misbehaviors such as dawdling, crying, and complaints of physical symptoms. To begin, the child should be required to rise from bed 90–120 minutes prior to entry into school. A child expected to enter the school building at 8:50 A.M., for example, might be expected to rise from bed at 6:50 A.M. Greater time should be allotted for youths who show many or intense misbehaviors in the morning.

Work with parents to divide the morning routine into individual components based on what a child must do to get ready for school. This usually involves, though not necessarily in this order, washing, dressing and accessorizing, eating breakfast, brushing teeth and hair, and making final preparations for school such as getting one's backpack or putting on one's jacket. Ask parents how long it should take their child to complete each activity and *then give extra time to allow the child to do so.* The extra time will serve as a buffer in case dawdling or other problems occur. So, if a child should take 10 minutes to eat breakfast but often takes 15 minutes after dawdling, assign 20 minutes to this task. The morning routine should be set but also

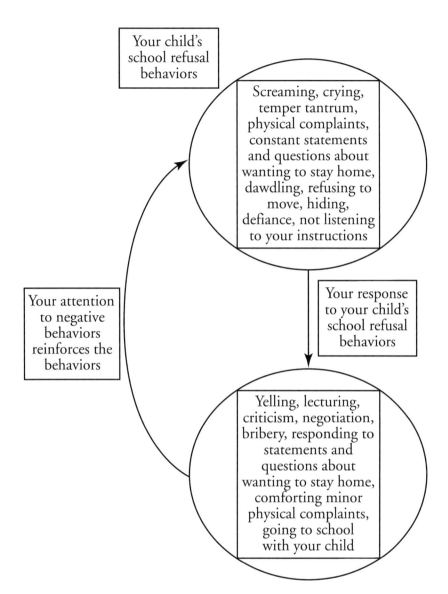

Figure 4.1.

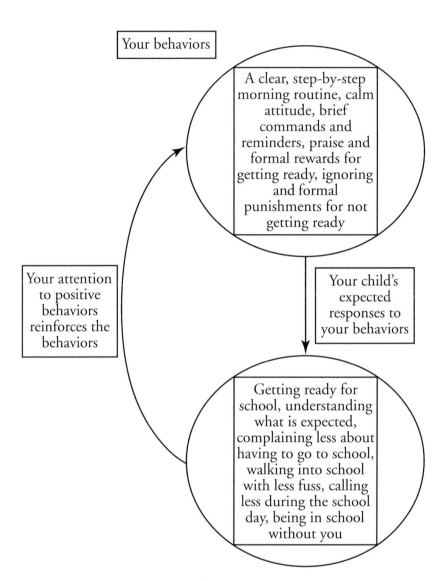

A clear, step-by-step morning routine, calm attitude, brief commands and reminders, praise and formal rewards for getting ready, ignoring and formal punishments for not getting ready

Your attention to positive behaviors reinforces the behaviors

Your child's expected responses to your behaviors

Getting ready for school, understanding what is expected, complaining less about having to go to school, walking into school with less fuss, calling less during the school day, being in school without you

Figure 4.2.

be flexible enough to absorb problems, thus reducing stress for the family. A sample morning routine follows:

6:50 A.M.	Rise from bed
6:50–7:00 A.M.	Go to the bathroom and wash (10 minutes)
7:00–7:20 A.M.	Eat breakfast (which should be ready by 7:00 or whenever breakfast time starts) (20 minutes)
7:20–7:30 A.M.	Brush teeth in bathroom and wash as needed (10 minutes)
7:30–7:50 A.M.	Dress and accessorize for school (20 minutes)
7:45–8:00 A.M.	Make final preparation for school such as putting on a jacket or getting one's backpack ready) (15 minutes)
8:00–8:20 A.M.	Extra time (if child is ready, provide some reward at this time; if child is not ready, he can use this time to finish) (20 minutes)
8:20–8:40 A.M.	Commute to school (20 minutes)
8:40–8:50 A.M.	Final good-byes and child enters school (10 minutes)

Work with parents as well to help a child rise from bed on time in the morning. If a child must rise from bed at 6:50 A.M., for example, then have parents assist the waking process at 6:30, 6:40, 6:45, and 6:48 A.M. Inform the child of the new waking and morning routine so he is not surprised by what will happen and knows what is expected of him. Do not allow a child to negotiate changes in the morning routine with you or his parents. The goal is to reestablish parent control during the morning routine and ensure that a child receives attention for appropriate school readiness behaviors. A worksheet for helping parents develop a morning routine is presented here (see Worksheet 4.1).

You must tailor the morning routine to the demands and constraints of an individual family. For example, one spouse may have to leave for work during the middle of the morning routine. In this case, accomplishing as much as possible before the spouse leaves or having another adult or older sibling assist in the morning routine might be desirable. Be sure as well to have the family "try out" the morning routine for a few days to see what needs tweaking, such as extra time for dressing. Finally, convey and emphasize to parents the *importance*

Worksheet 4.1

Our Morning Routine

What I Want My Child To Do	*Time to Complete this Step* (e.g., 7:00–7:20 A.M.)

of remaining consistent and persistent in the morning routine. The child must not come to believe that too much "wiggle room" exists during the course of the morning routine. As such, you should stay in close contact with parents during the early stages of this intervention to motivate them to continue and provide feedback on easing the process to increase parental compliance.

Attending to Appropriate Behaviors and Ignoring Inappropriate Behaviors

Once the morning routine is set, parents should actively attend to appropriate morning behaviors and ignore or downplay inappropriate behaviors. Many parents fall into the trap of attending to kids when they misbehave or cry and leaving children alone when they behave well. This pattern must be switched, especially in the morning. Begin by encouraging parents to focus on positive child behaviors in the morning, especially rising from bed on time and staying on schedule during the morning routine. It may be helpful also to encourage parents to *engage in the same tasks at the same time* with a child to increase attention and supervision. A parent could, for example, eat breakfast and brush teeth with his or her child. All of this serves to reinforce "good" child behavior. Remember that the key reinforcer for this group is attention. Therefore, smiles, words of praise, happy or goofy looks, touches, and hugs are often most useful.

In contrast, parents must downplay or ignore minor inappropriate behaviors such as dawdling, complaints about school or physical symptoms, and whining. Parents must convey to their children that school attendance is expected and that negotiation will not be tolerated. Parents should serve as a good role model in the morning by getting ready for the day themselves, minimizing attention to negative behaviors, and encouraging children to keep moving to get ready for school.

If a child complains of physical symptoms, then be sure a pediatrician has ruled out medical causes. Parents should expect to send a child to school unless a severe medical problem is present (see Chapter 3). Minor physical complaints should thus be downplayed. *As a general rule, parents must build the expectation that their child is to attend school without discussion.* The default option must always be school attendance.

Establishing Formal Rewards and Punishments for School Attendance/Nonattendance

For some children, like Eevie, simply attending to positive behaviors and downplaying or ignoring misbehaviors is not enough. In these cases, parents must establish *formal rewards* for school attendance and *formal punishments* for school refusal behavior and especially nonattendance. Again, with this group, the most effective kinds of rewards and punishments will be attention based.

Formal rewards for appropriate school attendance, or attendance without major problems such as temper tantrums, can include things such as staying up at night a little later than usual, doing fun activities with a parent, reading stories together, running errands together, or even taking a walk around the neighborhood to discuss the day. These are all rewards that can be done in the evening. In addition, parents should set aside some time after a successful morning routine to immediately reward a child. Using the morning routine previously outlined, a child who successfully completes this routine at 8:00 A.M. has 20 minutes of "free time." This reward time could involve a brief activity with a parent or general play. In this way, a child's school attendance is rewarded immediately as well as at night. Some children prefer more tangible rewards during this time, such as watching a favorite television show, and this is fine as well.

The flip side to all of this, of course, is what to do if a child actively refuses to engage in the morning routine or go to school. In this case, formal punishments must be established and administered in the morning, during school hours if the child remains home, *and* during the evening. Parents often make the mistake of "letting a child off the hook" in the evening following a child's morning misbehavior. Instead, children must understand that such misbehaviors will have serious consequences at night.

Parents should identify two or three main behavior problems in the morning and link specific punishments to these behaviors. In Eevie's case, we could identify temper tantrums and refusal to enter the school building as the two most serious school refusal behaviors to address. A good rule of thumb for parents to follow is this: *administer formal punishment in the evening for morning misbehaviors at the rate of twice the number of minutes a child actively refused school.* If a child threw a temper tantrum for 20 minutes on the school playground, for example, she would "owe" her parents 40 minutes of punishment time that night. If Eevie clung to her mother for 15 minutes before entering school, then she would "owe" her mother 30 minutes of punishment time that night. If a child dawdled in the morning and was late finishing a morning routine component by 4 minutes, then he would "owe" his parents 8 minutes of punishment time that night.

Formal punishments, as with rewards, should be attention based. Examples include going to bed early, sitting on the stairs or on one's bed away from family members, or losing a fun activity with a parent. More tangible punishments, such as loss of computer or television time, may be necessary as well. If a child amasses huge amounts of punishment time, she could spend the evening in her room or be allowed in the evening or on the weekend to finish a long, onerous chore such as helping with yard work to wipe the slate clean and start fresh the following week.

Parents must be discouraged from threatening extreme punishments such as canceling a major holiday or birthday because of non-attendance. *Instead, punishments must be basic and applied daily and consistently.* In addition, many parents in this population mishandle physical punishment, so I do not recommend this. Finally, as discussed in Chapter 3, if a child does remain home from school, attention toward the child should be minimized and he should be expected to complete homework provided by a teacher or complete other academic tasks. Formal punishments should then be given in the evening for failure to attend school.

Altering Parent Commands

Another clinic-derived strategy for parents is altering commands they give to their children. You may not have the time to do this with a parent, but perhaps a brief feedback session could be feasible. Parents of these kids may have fallen into the habit of bargaining or negotiating with their child or engaging in long lectures, diatribes, criticisms, sarcasm, and pleadings. In addition, many parents become so frustrated at their child's school refusal behavior that they yell or say hurtful things. As you might guess, none of this has worked and the child has retained control of the situation.

An alternative strategy is to change parent commands and tone of voice to help reestablish parent control. Because you may not have much time to interact with parents, providing them with some brief recommendations for appropriate parental commands might be helpful:

- Tell a child exactly what to do (instead of "clean your room," say "pick up all of your clothes off the floor right now").
- Give short, direct commands that involve only one step (the child can then come back to the parent for a second command).
- Make direct eye contact with a child when making a command so you know you have his full attention.
- Be sure a child can physically do what is asked of her.
- Do a task with a child to increase attention and supervision.
- Praise good listening and compliance, and discourage poor listening or noncompliance.

Parents must practice these behaviors during the day and especially in the morning before school. *In addition, encourage parents to be as matter-of-fact or neutral in their tone as possible.* My favorite line that I tell parents to say to their children is "You're going to school, end of story." This reinforces the expectation that a child is to attend school and that negotiation or bargaining is out of the question. The line can be used when a child whines or asks questions or makes statements about not wanting to attend school.

Addressing Excessive Reassurance-Seeking and Clingy Behavior

In line with the last point about responding to a child's inappropriate pleas to remain home from school, parents must know how to handle excessive reassurance-seeking and clingy behavior in their children. Excessive reassurance-seeking involves issuing the same questions or statements over and over to induce parental acquiescence to desires to remain home from school. Common questions children pester their parents with include "Do I really have to go to school today?" or "Can't I just stay home with you today?" Common statements include "I don't want to go to school" and "I want to stay home!"

These questions and statements, when done repeatedly, are exhausting for a parent to continually address. So I recommend placing a child on a "schedule" whereby their questions or statements are answered only after a set time period. A child who asks on a Sunday afternoon whether she can stay home from school tomorrow could be met with a parent's response that, yes, she is going to school. Subsequent questions or statements about refusing school are then ignored for at least one hour. In this way, constant questions and statements are not rewarded and parents do not spend so much energy addressing them. The "schedule" for responding can later be extended to two or three hours.

Another form of excessive reassurance-seeking behavior among youths who refuse school for attention is constant telephone calls to parents from school. In this case, I also recommend placing kids on a "schedule" whereby a single call to a parent is allowed if a child attended school successfully and was not disruptive in class. In addition, the telephone call should be at a time when most convenient for the school, such as during a child's lunch or recess time. Many school districts have policies against such calls, however, and so this must obviously be considered.

Excessive reassurance-seeking behavior can also come in the form of "clingy" behavior, such as what Eevie did on the playground before school. Many parents say they can get their child to the school grounds but then have great trouble getting her inside the building or into the classroom. In this situation, the following may be helpful:

- A parent should ensure that a child has everything necessary for the day (to avoid a child's suddenly "remembering" an item was forgotten and thus forcing a return trip home).
- A parent should arrive at the school playground at the same time each school day and preferably about 10 minutes before the child must enter the school building.
- A parent should walk the child to the playground or place where kids must line up to enter the building.
- A parent should minimize conversation with the child and ignore minor complaints, crying, statements about not wanting to attend, and other misbehaviors.
- A parent should say a final good-bye quickly and then leave quickly.
- You should meet the parent and child on the playground and courteously but quickly escort him to class. If possible, prevent the child from going toward his parent or allowing the parent to dawdle or take the child home.
- You should contact the parent later that morning to provide feedback on what transpired after the parent left (assuming the child successfully entered the school building or classroom).

Forcing School Attendance

If you find that none of what has been discussed so far is working, you may have to recommend physically forcing a child to attend school. *Forced school attendance should be done only as a last resort and only under very certain circumstances.* I recommend forced school attendance *only if all* of the following conditions apply: the child is younger than age 10, the child has no distress at all about attending school (see Chapter 3), the child is refusing school only for attention, the child understands fully what will happen if he refuses school, the child is missing more days than not, two adults can take the child to school, parents have the energy and no reservation about taking the child to school, and you or another school official knows what is scheduled to happen and meets the parents to escort the child to class quickly.

Forced school attendance begins during the morning routine when a child refuses to attend school. Parents first issue a warning that the child must attend school or he will be physically taken to school. If the latter is necessary, then two adults physically bring the child to the car as one drives and one remains in the back to supervise the child. School refusal behaviors such as tantrums or crying are ignored. Parents then bring the child to a waiting school official and leave quickly after depositing him at school. Parents and school officials can then speak during the morning to assess what happened and what may need to change.

A severe downside to forced school attendance is that if parents give up on the procedure, reintegrating a child to school in future days will be very difficult. The child has essentially "survived" the strongest intervention possible and will be more emboldened to resist other methods to increase school attendance. Therefore, this procedure should be used only as a last resort, if all of the above conditions apply, *and* if you are fully confident that parents and you or other school officials can sanction and follow through with the procedure.

Modifications for a School Setting

In an urgent situation or one when time is scarce, emphasizing the development of a structured morning routine is recommended. Parents often find it much easier to do the other things mentioned here, such as administering appropriate rewards and punishments, if things are set in the morning and all family members know what is expected. The predictability of a set morning routine is comforting to children as well. Another key intervention component to emphasize if time is short is punishment of school refusal behaviors in the evening. Children must come to understand that their misbehavior will not be forgotten and that school attendance is a top priority. Helping parents establish the default expectation or attitude that a child *will attend school even with minor problems* such as achiness or a case of the "sniffles" is also extremely important. Finally, the procedures discussed so far in this chapter obviously require extensive parent effort. If such effort is not present, then other modifications will have to be made (see Chapter 5).

Another modification of these procedures is to help parents teach their children to handle unpredictable situations. As mentioned earlier, many kids who refuse school for attention, like Eevie, demand that their parents pick them up at a certain time, and many parents carefully arrange their schedule to do so. You can help parents change this behavior by establishing a schedule whereby a child is picked up from school at different times during the week. A child who insists on being picked up at 3:22 P.M., for example, could be told she will be picked up any time between 3:15 and 3:35 P.M. She will be expected to wait outside for a parent and could be picked up on time or a bit earlier or a bit later (though no later than 3:35 P.M.). Initially, you could wait with the child to help her handle the unpredictable circumstance. Over time, the child should be able to handle different times on her own. As she does so, praise her ability to wait. This process helps reestablish parent control because parents dictate to a child what time range will apply instead of the child dictating a certain time that parents try to meet.

Youths Refusing School for Tangible Rewards Outside of School

Another function of school refusal behavior based on positive reinforcement is pursuit of tangible rewards outside of school. Recall from Alexander's case that he commonly left school to be with friends and do fun activities outside of school. Youths of this function are generally older, often in middle or high school. They are not particularly stressed about school, though they could be the longer they are out of school and the more pressure there is to return to full-time school attendance. Addressing youths who refuse school for tangible rewards outside of school requires a *concerted effort between school officials, parents, and the adolescent.* As mentioned earlier, major components of intervention for this group include increasing supervision, developing written contracts to boost incentives for school attendance, escorting a child from class to class, and teaching a child to refuse offers from others to miss school.

Providing a Rationale for Intervention

The general goal of intervention for youths of this function is to increase incentives for school attendance and decrease incentives (or increase disincentives) for school absences. Illustrate to parents how a child's absences are reinforced by specific fun activities outside of school and be sure to know and convey exactly what these activities are. A key strategy will be to restrict these fun activities and provide more appropriate incentives for attending school. In addition, because school refusal behavior in this group tends to be secretive, increased supervision of the child and frequent communication between parents and school officials are a must.

Adolescents are different from children, so the strategy for this function *will* necessarily involve some negotiation with the youth. However, you should attempt to have all family members, including the adolescent, commit to a long-term goal of full-time school attendance. You may also wish to commit to certain support services that will help a child succeed in school, make school less boring for him, or give him hope that the school year is not lost. Examples include providing tutoring services, rearranging classes and lunchtime, easing deadlines for makeup work, and creating opportunities for the youth to salvage some academic credit for the year.

Increasing Supervision of the Youth

The secretive nature of youths who pursue tangible rewards outside of school demands increased supervision to prevent the students from leaving school. Although perhaps difficult logistically, successful intervention for these cases usually requires:

- Identifying and proactively short-circuiting high-risk times during the school day when a child is most likely to leave the school campus.
- Having a child visit you during times he is most likely to be missing school.
- Using attendance logs a child must have each teacher sign.

- Knowing exactly where a youth is when he is out of school during school hours and returning him to school when found.
- Establishing immediate communication between you and a parent when a child is out of school.

Youths are likely to leave school around lunchtime, but each child is different, so learn when a particular child is most likely to leave. Many youths of this function meet with friends during breaks in classes before and after lunch. Identify what time of day a youth is most likely to leave school and arrange for you or another school official to shadow or otherwise prevent this from happening. Many youths simply follow others when missing school, so "short-circuit" this process by pulling a youth aside, letting him know you are watching, or encouraging him to stay in school.

In related fashion, you may wish to require a child to visit you in your office or somewhere in the school building during times he has been most likely missing school. In Alexander's case, you could require him to visit you at 1:00 P.M. and 2:30 P.M. each day to check in and prove he is indeed in school. Failure to do so would result in immediate notification of parents and specific consequences. As the child's attendance level improves, these visits could be made more infrequently. Parents could also place strategic telephone calls to their child during high-risk times to ensure that he is in school.

In addition, a child can be required to maintain an *attendance log* (see Worksheet 4.2). The child should be instructed to bring the log to the teacher at the end of each class for signature before proceeding to the next class. Doing so serves two key purposes. First, school attendance is actively monitored and the log serves as evidence that a child was actually in school (or not). Logs are important when deciding whether rewards for school attendance should be given (see later contract section). Missed or forgotten signatures count as absences. Second, attendance logs require daily student-teacher contact, so an absence will be more easily noticed by a teacher who can then report this to you as soon as possible.

When a youth does leave school, you or the parents should discover where the child is so you can take appropriate action. You may not have the resources to do this, but parents should try to find their child quickly and return her to school that afternoon if possible. Some schools have truant officers as well who could be contacted if a particular child is known to have left school. Encourage parents to

Worksheet 4.2

Daily Attendance Log

Class (Starting with First Period)	Teacher's Name	Teacher's Signature and Date
_____	_____	_____
_____	_____	_____
_____	_____	_____
_____	_____	_____
_____	_____	_____
_____	_____	_____
_____	_____	_____
_____	_____	_____
_____	_____	_____
_____	_____	

identify likely places a child could be as well as contact information for parents of friends the child may be with. I know this is very difficult, but a child who knows she will be tracked down and brought back to school will be less likely to leave school than a youth who knows there will be no serious supervision or consequences for her absenteeism.

Finally, parents and school officials must establish a regular and open line of communication so each party is informed of a child's absence *as soon as it is known.* A parent who knows a child left home early in the morning to be with friends, for example, should contact you or the school official in charge of the child's case. Similarly, if you know a particular child has left the school campus during the day, then parents should be informed immediately of this event. Open and immediate communication allows for the greater possibility that a child's absenteeism will be addressed sooner rather than later.

Contracts for School Attendance

Carefully supervising a child's attendance is critical for a strategy designed to increase incentives for going to school and decreasing incentives for missing school. This strategy centers on developing a contract between parents and a youth with school refusal behavior. A contract is a *written agreement* that outlines privileges a child may receive for certain appropriate behaviors or responsibilities. In addition, a contract may outline certain disincentives or punishments for failure to display certain appropriate behaviors. A contract is thus an agreement between parents and a child that *explicitly details* what will happen if a child shows or does not show a specific behavior.

In my clinic, contracts are initially developed for minor things such as household chores and then morning preparation behaviors. These initial contracts are designed to show families how to solve problems without conflict and encourage negotiation between parents and a child. In your educational setting, however, you are not likely to have time to develop these early contracts. Instead, you will likely have to go straight to contracts that target school attendance.

When drafting a contract, you should meet with the parents and child and have each party sit in a different room. This may not be feasible, however, so you may have to meet with everyone together. Speak with the child first (preferably without the parents present) to discover what tangible privileges or items he enjoys that could be part of the contract. Talking with a youth first also conveys that his viewpoint will be taken seriously and that you are not simply another adult telling him what to do. Ask the youth to commit to a pattern of full-time school attendance or, in more severe cases, to some level of attendance. In addition, ask the youth to suggest an arrangement whereby certain tangible items or privileges are linked to a certain amount of school attendance.

Following this discussion, ask parents the same questions about potential privileges and responsibilities. Discover their expectations for their child's school attendance as well. In addition, convey that the contract is not designed to "pay" a child for going to school, something he should be doing anyway. Instead, privileges a child receives will be for attending school *and* completing some task or chore at home. Encourage parents to develop *realistic* goals, rewards, and disincentives for the contract. This may mean encouraging parents to commit first to only a part-time attendance schedule for their child.

A sample contract is shown below. You can see that the contract lists specific privileges, responsibilities, and general statements that clearly define terms used in the agreement. When constructing a contract, be sure to adhere to the following rules:

- Contracts must be *written* to eliminate problems remembering what all parties must do.
- Contracts must be time limited and preferably no longer than one week in length.
- Everyone must completely agree with all contract provisions or the contract is invalid.
- Contract provisions must be within a family's value system and within their resources, so extravagant provisions must be avoided.
- Contract provisions must be very clearly defined.
- Contracts should be as simple and short as possible.

Once a contract is constructed and everyone agrees to its provisions, ask each party to sign the agreement and post it in an open area of the house. All parties should read the contract at least once per day. If possible, contact family members the next day to evaluate how the contract is progressing. Family members will tell you the contract worked well, someone did not fulfill his end of the

Sample Contract for Alexander

Privileges	*Responsibilities*
For the privilege of seeing his friends on the weekend,	Alexander agrees to have no more than zero marked absences this week.
For the privilege of being paid $10 for vacuuming the house on Saturday,	Alexander agrees to have no more than one marked class absence this week.
For the privilege of being paid $5 for vacuuming the house on Saturday,	Alexander agrees to have no more than two marked class absences this week.

General statements

A marked absence is equal to one missed class and is determined by the school.

"Vacuuming the house" means vacuuming the family room, living room, all bedrooms, and the stairs and landing. Mom will check to see that the vacuuming was done well.

If Alexander has one or more marked absences this week, he may not see his friends this weekend.

If Alexander has two or more marked absences this week, he must vacuum the house for free. If he does not vacuum the house, then he loses his computer, television, iPod, and telephone.

This contract is good only for this week (Monday-Friday).

Everyone who signs this contract agrees to the conditions of this contract and to read and initial the contract every day.

Child's signature: _____

Parent's signature(s): _____

Date: _____

contract, or the contract failed for some reason. In the first case, praise family members and ask them to continue with the contract. In the second case, urge a recalcitrant family member to discuss problems with the contract and rework the contract as necessary. If complete failure occurred, then rewrite the contract focusing on a shorter timeline, fewer expectations, or more intense rewards and sanctions. A contract should be designed for success, and this generally means one in which a youth is highly motivated to follow through with the agreement.

You may wish to start initial contracts with a part-time school attendance schedule (see examples in Chapter 3). Alexander, for example, could be required initially to attend school all morning and at least up to 1:30 P.M. each day. If the contract was successful, then Alexander's expected school attendance could involve a complete day. In some cases, a child wants the contract rewards but is still urged by others to miss school. Escorting a child from class to class and helping a youth refuse offers to miss school may thus be necessary. These two strategies are discussed next.

Escorting a Child From Class to Class

Contracts for increasing school attendance are effective but not if a child continues to have problems progressing from one class to the next. Many youths truly wish to adhere to a contract but cannot do so because of tempting offers to miss school. As a result, punishments from the contract are constantly administered and a youth's motivation to attend school suffers. To address this problem, I recommend two interventions: escorting a child from class to class, and helping youths actively refuse offers from others to miss school.

We certainly want a child to access rewards from the contract, so escorting him from class to class is a good way to ensure attendance and thereby ensure that he receives the benefits of doing so. Even though a child may be escorted from class to class, it still counts as attendance that should be rewarded in accordance with a contract. The primary issues to be decided, of course, is who will do the escorting and how.

If school resources are strained, the best option is to convince a family member to escort the youth from class to class. Parents are an obvious choice, but many cannot or will not do so. In this case, extended family members such as a grandparent or close family friends could be enlisted. If several people can escort the child from class to class, a rotating schedule could be developed. Downsides of this approach are that an outside adult must always be available for escorting, that withdrawing the escort may lead to a relapse toward absenteeism, and that outside escorts may conflict with school policy.

A better option, if school resources are available, is to have school officials conduct the escorting. This could be done in one of several ways. First, a peer monitor could escort the child and report to you any problems that result. If the child missed school, the peer monitor could also contact him at night to talk and encourage him to attend school the next day. Second, an adult school official could conduct the escorting, though this may be difficult. Third, each teacher could escort the child from the end of one class to the beginning of another. A child's first-period teacher, for example, could escort a child to the second-period class. The child's second-period teacher then walks her to her third-period class, and so forth throughout the day.

Escorting works well but is obviously time-consuming. Therefore, escorting should boost school attendance and subsequence rewards before being scaled back to see whether a child can attend school more independently. One "scale back" option is to limit escorting to high-risk times of the day, such as after a child's lunch to his sixth-period class. Youths who complain about escorts can be reminded that demonstrating regular school attendance is expected and will lead to less supervision. Youths should also understand that future unexcused absences can result in resumed escorting.

Helping Youths Refuse Offers to Miss School

Another way to help youths stay in school and receive contract rewards is to teach them how to refuse offers from others to miss school. In essence, a child needs to know *what he can do or say to avoid situations that tempt him to miss school or decline offers in a socially acceptable way.* In Alexander's case, he could be encouraged not to go to his locker at 11:30 A.M. because that is when many of his friends congregate and discuss whether to miss school. In some cases, lunchtimes or class schedules can be rearranged so a child finds it easier to avoid peers likely to badger him to miss school.

Of course, avoiding certain people and places is not foolproof. Therefore, youths must also have skills to rebuff direct offers from others to miss school. However, whatever statements they make to their friends must be delicate enough that the child is not embarrassed or made to look foolish. In addition, a child should make statements that are clear and reasonable to others. Simply saying "I don't want to go," for example, is not likely to be an effective response.

Help a child develop *specific statements* to refuse offers to miss school. A child can blame others, such as you or his parents, for example, by saying "My parents and the guidance counselor are giving me a hard time about going to school" or "They're all watching me closely and I don't want detention." Or, the child can allude to something in the contract and say "I have to stay in school this week if I want to hang with you guys Friday night." A youth can also talk about wanting to finish certain school projects or attend an extracurricular activity. Alternatively, kids can be encouraged to simply say nothing and walk away in some cases.

Youths also commonly report concern about what to say to peers and others if they have been out of school for some time and are now returning. I have treated many youths very concerned about their first day back after having missed much school. These youths are most worried about questions such as "Where have you been?" and "Why did you miss so much school?" In these scenarios, recommend that the youth provide brief and accurate though not overly informative answers. Examples include "I was having trouble going but now I'm back!" or "I was having a lot of fun but have to work hard now," or "I wasn't feeling up to going to school but I'm ready for school now."

Modifications for a School Setting

Contracts are wonderful tools for motivating kids to return to school but, admittedly, they take a lot of work. You may find it necessary to quickly arrange some kind of agreement, even if over the telephone and oral in nature. Oral contracts are susceptible to selective "forgetting" and misinterpretation, but sometimes this is the best you will be able to do. An oral contract is better than no contract at all, however, so try hard to get some agreement in place. Keep in mind that an oral contract will require even more follow-up and encouragement from you to help the youth stay on task. You should write down the provisions of an oral contract so if a family dispute does take place, a telephone call or e-mail to you can quickly resolve the conflict.

Encourage parents and the child to meet frequently, at least once per evening for a few minutes, to discuss the contract or oral agreement, potential obstacles that might impede the contract/agreement, and whatever offers were made to the child that day from others to miss school. Discussions can also surround escorting schedules and how rewards and punishments can be modified to make a contract/agreement even stronger. Encourage parents to frequently praise their child's attendance.

This function is perhaps the most difficult to treat because of the intense conflict, frustration, and dismissiveness of many parents who have dealt with a child's intense and secretive school refusal behavior for many years. As a result, this function may be the one for which you are most likely to recommend adjunct therapy in addition to your attempts to resolve a child's school refusal behavior. For example, a therapist may help a family develop better communication and problem-solving skills and reduce bitterness among its members. If a child in this function also displays severe delinquent behavior or if parents show psychopathology themselves, then referral to a therapist to address these issues is important as well.

Final Comments and What's Next

Chapters 3 and 4 discussed clinic-derived strategies for addressing youths refusing school for negative or positive reinforcement. Although modifications of these procedures for school settings were outlined, other larger variables often impact this population and are seen especially by school officials. The remaining chapters of this book are designed to help school officials address some of these larger issues. Chapter 5, for example, talks about interactions with difficult parents as well as special issues that apply to the functions of school refusal behavior. Chapter 6 covers more preventive and systemic strategies for school refusal behavior. Chapter 7 covers larger contextual issues that can impact school attendance and how school officials can address these variables.

5

Difficult Parents and Other Special Topics

Colby is a 14-year-old boy in ninth grade who has missed several days of school this semester. Colby has a long history of school refusal behavior dating to the beginning of middle school. An assessment reveals that Colby is missing school for tangible rewards outside of school, including time spent with friends, as well as to avoid general distress about school. Discussions with Colby's parents about this issue have been difficult. Colby's parents vociferously blame school officials for Colby's absenteeism and for failing to inform them of the severity of their son's problem. Although Colby's parents seemed invested in resolving their son's school refusal behavior the last two years, they seem much less invested this year. This is evidenced by failure to return telephone calls or appear for scheduled appointments with Colby's guidance counselor.

Sarah is an 11-year-old girl in sixth grade with tremendous anxiety about attending school and interacting with other children. Her parents are fairly strict and require Sarah to come home right after school. She is not permitted to attend extracurricular activities and often seems socially withdrawn at school. Sarah's parents have been reluctant to discuss their daughter's "problem" and have implied that the school is to blame. They are considering home schooling as an option because their daughter seems so distressed, especially on Sunday evenings prior to a school week.

The procedures discussed in Chapters 3 and 4 are effective ways of helping youths such as Colby and Sarah return to school with less distress. However, the "real world" impinges greatly on cases of school refusal behavior, and school officials are commonly faced with special challenges. Many therapists, for example, do not have to worry as much about parent motivation because parents have already made the decision to attend therapy and try to resolve a child's school refusal behavior. You obviously do not always have this luxury and are often faced with parents like those of Colby and Sarah.

This chapter covers difficult parents and other special topics that impinge upon treatment for the four functions of school refusal behavior emphasized in previous chapters. The topic of "difficult parents" is addressed first because this issue affects all functions and is one that concerns many school officials. Other special topics tend to be more specific to certain functions, however, so a discussion of these topics has been arranged accordingly.

Difficult Parents

What do I mean by "difficult parents?" Difficult parents are generally combative, dismissive, or confused about a child's school refusal behavior. *Combative parents* may blame you or other school officials for a child's problem or are angry they have not been sufficiently informed of their child's absenteeism (even when evidence to the contrary is presented to them). Combative parents may balk at whatever solutions you propose, act defensively, or threaten administrative, legal, or other action such as removing their child from school. Many combative parents give you detailed reasons to show that what you are proposing will not work. These parents may be hostile, defiant, skeptical, suspicious, evasive, and pessimistic about change. In essence, these parents seem determined to challenge you every step of the way.

Dismissive parents seem relatively unconcerned about their child's absenteeism, are lackadaisical about discipline, or fail to respond to your overtures for resolving a child's school refusal behavior. Like Colby's parents, they do not show up for appointments, return telephone calls or e-mails, or even seem to want to be found in some cases. Some dismissive parents are overly permissive in their discipline or do not care to intervene in a child's problem unless the situation is dire. These problems may extend to other school-related areas as well, such as attending parent-teacher conferences, supervising homework, or enforcing appropriate bedtimes. These parents may prefer "quick fixes," rely too much on your efforts to return a child to school, unnecessarily

delay intervention, or fear their child may be harmed by school attendance. Other dismissive parents claim they did just fine despite their
own limited school attendance. School officials commonly lament that
some parents simply do not value education.

Confused parents have great problems understanding their child's
school refusal behavior and what you want them to do to resolve the
situation. These parents may be tangential in their thinking or have
trouble maintaining regular conversations without telling some irrelevant story or conveying unrelated information. Other confused
parents are beset by intense marital or financial problems, domestic
violence, psychopathology, or family dysfunction and simply cannot
focus on their child's school refusal behavior. Of course, difficult parents could also involve a combination of combativeness, dismissiveness, and confusion.

To make matters even more complicated, difficult parents may
intersect with problematic family dynamics common to youths with
school refusal behavior:

- *Conflictive family members* often argue and fight with one another
  and generally have poor problem-solving and communication skills.
- *Enmeshed family members* are over-involved with each other's lives
  and may have trouble separating from one another.
- *Isolated family members* rarely interact with people outside the family unit, including school officials (as with Sarah's parents).
- *Detached family members* are relatively uninterested in each other's
  lives, which may lead to lax discipline and poor supervision.
- *Mixed dynamics* include some combination of these family dynamics.

*Not all youths who refuse school have difficult parents or problematic
family dynamics.* Many children distressed about school come from
healthy family dynamics and two parents highly motivated to resolve
the problem. In addition, a single parent may present some challenges
with respect to resources available to address her child, but she may
still be enthusiastic about solving a school refusal problem. For those
cases where you are faced with difficult parents or problematic family
dynamics, however, the following ideas may be helpful.

Increase Collaborative Contact

Parents most commonly complain to me that school officials are uninterested in their child's problem or fail to provide them with critical

information about their child's school refusal behavior. They also commonly complain that school officials adopt a threatening and defensive approach during conversations about their child. This is not necessarily true, of course. In many cases, school officials have clearly and repeatedly tried to work with parents to resolve an absentee problem. Still, many cases of school refusal behavior involve, for whatever reason, intense parent–school official tension, friction, or conflict.

As difficult as it may be, having frequent contact with parents is important. This contact could be in the form of daily telephone calls, e-mails, progress notes, or other methods (see Chapter 2). *Parents are generally more receptive to school officials if they know a child's absenteeism is tracked at school and if school officials let them know immediately about unexcused absences.* Chapters 3 and 4 discussed different intervention techniques that require frequent and bilateral parent–school official feedback. The more frequent your contact with parents, even difficult ones, the better your chances of resolving a child's school refusal behavior. For parents difficult to locate, registered mailings, home visits, or contacts with family friends or relatives may be necessary.

Frequent contact with parents will obviously include information about your intervention *and* detailed rationales for immediately and intensely implementing your plan. Family members should be well informed of the dangers of ongoing absenteeism, including declining grades, risk of school dropout, reduced opportunities for socialization, family conflict, and legal and disciplinary consequences. Ongoing communication about the following topics is important as well:

- A child's recent school absences (frequency, type, pattern, function).
- A child's course schedule and grades.
- A child's current homework and required makeup work.
- A child's current behavior in school, including level of distress, interactions with peers and others, and behavior problems.
- School rules about attendance, student conduct, and leaving the school campus early.
- Expected timeline and obstacles for getting a child back to school.

When speaking to difficult parents, emphasize a nondefensive, collaborative approach. Even if you strongly feel parents are to blame for a child's absenteeism, conveying this thought will only damage the resolution process. Instead, emphasize the need for a positive working relationship between you and parents that must involve trust and great effort from both parties. Be neutral and matter-of-fact in your tone and listen carefully to what a parent says. Many parents need to "vent" for several minutes before reaching a mood in which they can collaborate to solve an absentee problem. You may have to "weather the storm" in some cases before focusing on what can be done in the next few days to help a child return to school. Try to steer the conversation away from past events *to what can be done in the next few days.* Emphasize how you and the parent can work together to resolve a child's school refusal behavior.

Difficult parents often respond well to even minor improvements over a short period of time. Try to focus on a very short-term approach of what can be done in the next 3–4 days. If a child or parent shows even some improvement, praise parents for their efforts and point out how your collaborative relationship facilitated some change. If you can show evidence of improvement, then parents generally become less frantic and more motivated to continue doing what is needed to maintain progress. Evidence of improvement may be in the form of better attendance, completed work, test scores, and school-based behavior.

Parents are also commonly frustrated by the extensive bureaucracy of a school system, so I recommend assigning one school official as a "point person" for their child's case. The point person can serve as a parent's primary contact and the person who can best cut through red tape and act as a parent's advocate within the school system. The point person could also be the one person other school officials contact for information about a child's school refusal behavior and intervention. When parents know there is someone they can readily contact for help and feedback, their motivation to collaborate increases greatly.

Meet at School or Home if Possible

Many parents feel frustrated by telephone conversations with school officials or cannot or will not meet a school official in their office. In these cases, it may be necessary to personally meet with parents at school or within their home. Face-to-face contact within the school setting is important for several reasons. One, meeting in person allows you to develop better rapport with family members. Two, parents are more likely to collaborate on your proposed intervention in person than over the telephone. Three, bringing a child to school for a meeting serves as a "mini-exposure" to the school setting. While the child is there, he can refamiliarize himself with aspects of school such as the classrooms, cafeteria, and hallways. Four, meeting in person conveys the message that a child's school refusal behavior is taken seriously and that you are invested in resolving the situation.

Another strategy when addressing difficult parents is to work closely with professionals from other legal or social agencies a family is involved with. Many families of this population currently meet with professionals from social service agencies, mental health clinics, juvenile justice systems, and other organizations. You could work closely with another professional who has already established good rapport with the family. In addition, you might be able to schedule a weekly family meeting with both professionals (you and the other person) at school to help parents solve various problems simultaneously, provide financial and legal resources, and ensure everyone is "on the same page" with respect to your proposed intervention for absenteeism. This kind of "one-stop shopping" is easier for parents and helps coordinate plans for that week. Difficult parents sometimes become more responsive when they understand that school-based intervention can be tailored to help them address various problems and not simply absenteeism. This is especially the case if parents know others are available to help them address home-based as well as school-based behavior problems.

Meeting family members in their home is another option but obviously one that depends on time, legal, and safety concerns. However, many parents respond positively to such visits. Home visits may be especially important in cases in which family members have cultural concerns about sending a child to school. Some parents are reluctant to send a child to school if doing so means the child might stray from important family and cultural values. Meeting family members in their home may produce a sense of reassurance and an action plan about these issues that can facilitate a child's return to school (see also Chapter 7). Home visits may be preferable as well in cases where families have poor transportation, economic hardships, lack of babysitting, and reduced motivation to visit the school.

Give Information About Options

Parents commonly complain that school officials are unreceptive to alternative plans to resolve their child's school refusal behavior. For example, they often grumble that school officials provide them with only two extreme options: get the child to attend school on a full-time basis immediately, or face referral for legal action. Because neither option is necessarily possible or palatable, parents may become hostile or uncooperative and withdraw from the problem-solving process.

Provide parents with as many options as possible. Some of these options, such as developing 504 or individualized education plans, are discussed later in this chapter. Other options include vocational educational settings, alternative high schools, part-time instructional or partial credit programs, after school or summer courses, credit-by-examination or equivalency diploma procedures, and school-based mental health services to improve school attendance. Each school district offers different programs, of course, so be knowledgeable about what programs exist in yours and which might be best for a particular child with school refusal behavior. Help parents pursue one or more of these options as appropriate and monitor the child's progress. Educational options are usually more diverse and available for high school students than middle or elementary school students. For nonadolescents, plans to reintegrate a child to her regular classroom setting will likely have to be emphasized.

Simplify Intervention Procedures

School officials and therapists commonly lament that parents do not follow through on elaborate plans designed to help a child return to school, even after family members have committed strongly to the plan! In many cases, parents often have good intentions but simply lack energy, time, or skills to implement a complicated intervention. In these cases, simplifying the intervention is a must. If a child is truly distressed about school, for example, parents may be unable to help their child simultaneously address all three aspects of anxiety discussed in Chapter 3. Instead, they might be able to first address only the physical component by focusing on relaxation. Only later might they be able to gradually reintroduce their child to a regular classroom. In other cases, a child's reintegration to school will necessarily have to be very slow.

If you must simplify an intervention, work with other school officials to inform them of the intervention and its progress as well as efforts family members are making to bring a child back to school.

In addition, you may wish to develop a 504 or individualized education plan, delay referral for legal action, adjust class schedules and assigned teachers, seek administrative permission for an initial part-time attendance schedule, and work toward giving a child a realistic chance to pass the school year or obtain partial credit. It is also helpful to develop a plan to accommodate substantial makeup work awaiting a child upon his return to school. This may involve easing the timeline for completing this work or arranging with teachers some alternative method of achieving a passing grade.

Explore and Defuse Potential Obstacles to an Intervention

In addition to simplifying an intervention, explore possible obstacles. I commonly ask parents, after they have agreed to a wonderful intervention plan, what could possibly go wrong. I am always surprised by the number of potential problems they raise, but *all potential problems must be addressed before the intervention begins.* Often these problems include lack of spousal or other adult support, parent guilt, transportation difficulties, poor energy, and lack of motivation or parent supervision. Reasons for noncompliance are many, but identifying these reasons and providing solutions is crucial. Possible solutions may involve sending school personnel to a child's house to transport her to school, arranging taxi rides to school, mobilizing a family's social support network, providing financial and other resources to help parents implement an intervention, and resolving school-based conflicts with teachers, peers, and others.

In cases of school withdrawal (see Chapter 1), you will have to adjust your intervention to account for extraneous problems such as custody disputes or maltreatment or provide incentives for participation in your intervention. Another school withdrawal obstacle you may face is a parent who feels guilty, nervous, or fearful of sending or "forcing" her child to school. This may be due to parent separation anxiety, overprotectiveness, or unjustified worry about the school setting. These parents may also sabotage a child's attendance by asking leading questions such as "Are you sure you really want to go to school today?" In this case, provide a parent with information about the difference between appropriate and inappropriate firmness, reassure a parent of a child's safety at school, focus on the rationale and goals of intervention (such as reestablishing parent control), have parents pursue a medical examination to rule out physical causes of symptoms, and maintain frequent and warm contact with parents.

Be aware as well that many children *increase the severity of their school refusal behavior* after parents begin to implement an intervention. Increased misbehavior is often designed to force parents to acquiesce to demands for school nonattendance or maintain the status quo. Parents must be prepared for this ambush by *knowing exactly how to respond to all possible misbehaviors in the morning and during the day.* In addition, I strongly recommend speaking to parents frequently after initial implementation of an intervention to encourage them to adhere to the plan and make subtle changes to accommodate a child's increased misbehavior.

Noncompliance with your intervention can also come from *school officials.* School staff members may insist that a disruptive child be sent home during the day, be openly hostile toward a child, engage in poor record keeping, fail to supervise a child's behavior or attendance, assign a child to inappropriate class or work placements, or deliberately fail a child academically. In these cases, you may wish to include certain staff members when developing your intervention to boost their input and level of cooperation. In addition, convey the importance of keeping daily and accurate records of behavior, ask staff members to send a child to your office instead of home, remove obstacles to good supervision, and frequently review a child's behavioral and academic status. As mentioned earlier, finding ways to salvage the school year is also important. In extreme cases of student-teacher conflict, consider changes in teachers or class schedule.

Single Parents

As mentioned earlier, single parents are not necessarily difficult parents. Many, indeed, are not. However, single parents do present special challenges not always evident for dual-parent families. The most striking challenge is lack of resources with respect to time, finances, and energy. Single parents are often working two jobs, forced to leave home before a child must attend school, or unable to regularly meet school officials.

The most important advice I can give about single parents is to help them mobilize and perhaps expand their social support network. Single parents will often have to rely on help from an ex-spouse, grandparents, extended family members, neighbors, friends, fellow church parishioners, and even school officials to ease the morning routine and get a child to school (especially if multiple children are involved). Many kids in this population will attend school if someone constantly prods them to do so or if someone drives them to school to avoid the bus. Having other people available to help a child prepare for school in the morning and take a child to school will also convey to the child that school attendance is valued and always expected. Pressure will also ease on the single parent who may then have more energy to address other concerns.

Explore the Need for a Referral

Some parents or families are extremely dysfunctional or racked by severe marital conflict, domestic violence, or psychopathology such as substance abuse, depression, and anxiety disorders. In other cases, a family member or a child is suicidal or some horrendous trauma has occurred. In these cases, resolving a child's school refusal behavior may not be the most important or urgent goal. For some families, referral to mental health services is required first. Information regarding ways of locating psychologists, psychiatrists, or other mental health professionals who may be helpful in these situations can be found in Chapter 1. You should also know which local hospitals have inpatient units and which facilities will visit a child's home to conduct an assessment of dangerous behavior.

School officials may wonder what questions they or parents should pose to a potential therapist when referring a family for treatment. If a case involves school refusal behavior, you and/or parents should ask the following:

- What is your status as a provider? For example, are you a licensed clinical psychologist, board-certified psychiatrist, or unlicensed practitioner?
- What is your theoretical orientation and educational background, especially with respect to school refusal behavior?
- What types of problems do you specialize in addressing, and do you commonly see cases of school refusal behavior?
- If you do see cases of school refusal behavior, what is your common practice for consulting and working with school officials? Will you be willing to meet with school officials and parents at the school and consult on a regular, even daily, basis?

- What is the nature of assessment and therapy you do for school refusal behavior and related family problems?
- What are your fees and hours, and do you offer sliding-scale fees (based on a family's ability to pay) for those with limited financial resources or several dependents?

School refusal behavior can be a complicated problem to address, so make referrals to mental health professionals with experience working with these cases *and* who are willing and able to consult frequently with relevant school officials.

If All Else Fails

Some parents are, of course, simply unreachable or too unmotivated or belligerent to serve as collaborative partners in resolving a child's absenteeism. In these cases, more severe options must be pursued in accordance with school policies and legal mandates. This may mean referral to a juvenile justice or other legal system to pursue charges of educational neglect, truancy, or whatever statute applies. *If possible, use this option only as a last resort.* You will generally find parents to be more cooperative if they know they can do something to avoid legal complications.

Even if you eventually must refer a child and his parents to a legal system, be sure to provide substantial information about the legal process to family members. In my experience, parents appreciate knowing exactly what will happen as they progress through the legal system. The process obviously differs across jurisdictions, but common practices include appearing before a judge, meeting with juvenile detention or probation officers, arranging community service, and pursuing follow-up contact with school officials. Become knowledgeable of what will happen to family members following your referral to a legal system and provide this knowledge as well as support to them. In many cases, an absentee problem will come "full circle" when a judge mandates a collaborative process between you and the parents. Developing and maintaining rapport even after referral to a legal system will thus facilitate any remediation plan you propose.

The following sections of this chapter cover other special topics loosely arranged by function. Though most generally apply to one specific function, this is not always the case. Therefore, it is best to read each section.

Special Topics for Anxiety-Based Absenteeism

As discussed in Chapter 3, interventions for youths who refuse school for negative reinforcement address physical, cognitive, and behavioral components of distress or anxiety. Youths of this group are sometimes faced with unique challenges and concerns, or parents of these youths often have questions about topics specific to this function.

Medication

Parents and school officials often ask about medicating a child with school refusal behavior, especially one with intense general or social anxiety. The research literature is sparse regarding medication for youths with school refusal behavior, though some researchers have investigated antianxiety and antidepressant drugs for this population. Researchers have concentrated on antidepressants such as imipramine (Tofranil), fluoxetine (Prozac), fluvoxamine (Luvox), sertraline (Zoloft), and paroxetine (Paxil). Response rates to these medications are mixed among youths who refuse school, in part because these kids often show ambiguous and fluctuating symptoms (see Chapter 1).

Medication may be effective for certain youths with school refusal behavior more so than others. Adolescents tend to respond better than children because their symptoms are more crystallized and similar to those of adults. In addition, antidepressants are likely more effective for youths with school refusal behavior *and* depression. Youths with better attendance rates and less social and separation anxiety also do better on antidepressant medication. Antianxiety medications may be more effective for youths with intense rather than mild levels of distress. In general, medications may be more effective for older adolescents with severe anxiety or depression that accompanies their school refusal behavior. If you think medication might be helpful for a youth, especially before starting a reintegration schedule, then refer the family to a child psychiatrist who can prescribe appropriate medication and who can monitor potentially intense side effects.

Home Schooling

Some parents are so frustrated by their child's school refusal behavior, as in Colby's case, that they consider home schooling or home-based instruction as an option. In these cases, a child may be taught at home by a parent, educator, or other adult in accordance with a predetermined curriculum. Although home schooling has been traditionally reserved for youths with severe medical or other conditions that preclude formal school attendance, parents increasingly see home schooling as a viable method of educating their children. Benefits of home schooling include enhanced parent supervision, involvement in a child's education, and parent-child contact.

For youths with a history of school refusal behavior, I do not recommend home schooling as an option for three main reasons. First, parents who pursue home schooling simply to reduce a child's distress about school or attention-seeking behavior are rewarding a child's avoidance or desire to remain home. For the latter group, children retain control of the situation by forcing parents to attend to them. Second, youths in home schooling may be deprived of greater opportunities to build social skills, master anxiety in social situations, learn to perform well before others, and develop friendships. This is especially worrisome for youths who refuse school to escape aversive social and/or evaluative situations. Third, parents will likely find it extremely difficult to reintegrate a child to a regular classroom setting if she has been taught at home for some period of time.

If you speak to parents considering home schooling for a youth with a history of school refusal behavior, it is important to explore fully the pros and cons of this strategy. Focus on techniques described in Chapters 3 and 4 and the remainder of the book to gradually ease a child into a regular classroom setting with less distress. If parents decide on home schooling anyway, as some do simply to finish a particular academic year, then work closely with them to establish a reintegration schedule for the following year. In the meantime, ask a child to be in the school building on a regular basis, either to meet with you or perhaps attend an extracurricular activity. This helps maintain some social contact and familiarity with the school setting that may facilitate future reintegration.

School Bus Problems

Some children have little trouble entering and attending the school building but cannot abide the school bus. This may be due to fear of becoming ill, worry about seeing someone else become ill, nervousness about approaching school, or other reasons. In other cases, trouble riding the school bus is simply part of a larger attendance issue. In either case, using the gradual reintegration process discussed in Chapter 3 applies here.

I recommend that children adhere to a schedule whereby school bus riding is gradually increased. Steps in this process must initially involve a parent who supervises a child getting on the bus and then drives behind the bus for a short distance. Later steps involve greater child independence. Each step of the reintegration process should include relaxation and breathing techniques (see Chapter 3) to quell physical symptoms of anxiety. A child should not progress to the next step until her anxiety level is 2–3 on a 0–10 scale (see Chapter 2). Possible steps, in order from first to last, include the following:

- Child stands at the school bus stop, gets on the bus, walks around the bus, and exits the bus before a parent drives her to school.
- Child stands at the bus stop and rides to the next bus stop as a parent drives behind the bus; the child exits the bus at the next stop and rides the remaining way with the parent.
- Child stands at the bus stop and rides to the next two bus stops before exiting and riding the remainder of the way with a parent (riding gradually increases with respect to number of bus stops until the child can ride the bus independently all the way to school with a parent driving behind the bus).
- A parent drives away from the school bus 5 minutes before the bus arrives at school.
- Working backward, a parent drives away from the school bus 10, 15, 20 minutes, and then so forth until the child can ride the school bus to school without parent escort.

Sunday Evening Anxiety

Many kids distressed about school have substantial anxiety on Sunday night prior to the school week. These kids have what I call "Tom Sawyer" syndrome:

> Monday morning found Tom Sawyer miserable. Monday morning always found him so—because it meant another week's slow suffering at school. He generally began that day with wishing he had had no intervening holiday, it made the going into captivity and fetters again so much more odious. (Mark Twain, *The Adventures of Tom Sawyer*)

Sunday evenings (and Monday mornings) are difficult for some anxious kids because they, like Tom Sawyer, consider the entire school week instead of one day at a time. Sunday evening anxiety can happen any time during your intervention. It can be helpful for parents to schedule a fun family activity on Sunday afternoon but ensure that Sunday evening is quiet and restful. The goal here is to lower a child's physical arousal as much as possible on Sunday evening. Relaxation and proper breathing (see Chapter 3) may be helpful during this time. Parents should have a relaxed discussion with their child about his concerns but also make clear that school attendance is expected the next day.

Ask parents to help their child focus *only on Monday* and not the entire week. Some parents promise their children something fun on Friday night if the school week goes well but, for these kids, it's best to simply focus on Monday. Parents should plan something fun, albeit small, on Monday night so the child has something immediate to look forward to. This can involve a later bedtime, game or other fun activity with a parent, special dessert after dinner, or some other treat. In addition, parents should praise their child for Monday attendance and show their appreciation for his bravery and effort.

Panic Attacks

Parents occasionally say their child has anxiety or "panic" attacks in school. In most of these cases, the child is extremely distressed about school, may show many physical and cognitive symptoms of anxiety, and avoid school for hours or days. Although these episodes are upsetting and must be addressed, they are not necessarily panic attacks. A panic attack is a *10–15-minute episode* of very intense physical feelings such as increased heart rate, sweating, shaking, hot flashes, shortness of breath, nausea, and dizziness. Panic attacks usually involve thoughts of dying, losing control, going crazy, or being humiliated as well. *Panic attacks begin and end suddenly, so a child distressed about school for several hours is not likely having a panic attack.* Youths with extended but moderate anxiety will benefit from procedures discussed in Chapter 3.

Panic attacks themselves are harmless but obviously quite terrifying. They are more likely to occur in older adolescents and can lead to avoidance of many public situations, especially those associated with the possibility of another panic attack. If you address a youth who does seem to have panic attacks, refer him to a clinical child psychologist who specializes in the cognitive-behavioral treatment of anxiety disorders (see Chapter 1). Treatment of panic attacks generally involves helping a person manage physical symptoms of anxiety, modify irrational thoughts about the dangerous nature of the symptoms, and reduce avoidance of public situations. Medication may also be used as a primary or adjunct treatment in severe cases.

Being Teased

Kids anxious about school are also generally sensitive about being teased by other children. The best ways of responding to teasing include laughing or immediately "turning the tables" on the teaser with a witty comeback. Many anxious kids, however, do not have the temerity or wherewithal to make these kinds of responses. Therefore, it is best to recommend that the child simply ignore teasing and walk away as quickly as possible. In this case, the teaser is not rewarded with a response and will hopefully give up. In addition, encourage a child to use the breathing technique from Chapter 3 and seek the company of friends or others. A child should know as well which school official to approach if teasing becomes chronic or severe. Should mild teasing turn into bullying, this issue must obviously be addressed as well (see Chapter 7).

Perfectionism

Youths who refuse school for negative reinforcement occasionally display high levels of perfectionism or a need to be perfect in areas such as academics, appearance, or athletics. For some kids who refuse school, perfectionism about academics is a key reason. Many of these kids refuse to enter class, hand in homework, or perform before others because of intense fear of making mistakes. Making mistakes is sometimes associated with severe humiliating or otherwise aversive consequences such as school failure, social exclusion, or parent anger and disappointment.

Assuming these consequences are not realistic, perfectionist children should *practice making mistakes* to realize that the consequences of doing so are not dire. As with generally distressed children, concentrate on physical, cognitive, and behavioral aspects of perfectionism. Help a child manage physical symptoms of anxiety and focus on mental errors he may be making about mistakes. A good strategy for the latter is to inquire about the "worst-case scenario" for making a mistake and discuss how realistic or probable that scenario is. For example, a child may claim that three errors on a math worksheet will lead to a failing grade and grounding from parents. Feedback from the child's math teacher and parents may then be used to debunk this thought.

Most important, a child must attend classes despite the prospect of making mistakes. A child may be asked to deliberately practice making mistakes on written or other work to obtain evidence that dire consequences will not occur. However, refusal to attend school or hand in completed homework, no matter what state it is in, should be dealt with appropriately (see Chapter 4). If parents are perfectionists themselves, they may need feedback about how their expectations affect their child and that they must continue to encourage their child to attend school.

Gym Class

Physical education class is a difficult class to attend for many youths, particularly those highly anxious or sensitive about dressing or performing athletically before others. Teenagers in particular are naturally egocentric and worried about others' judgments, and these concerns seem aggravated in a setting in which one might be ridiculed, leered at, embarrassed, or picked last for a team. Many kids, like David in Chapter 3, thus decide to skip physical education or try to avoid as much participation as possible.

If you confront a youth with great difficulty attending physical education class, the following may prove helpful:

- Have the child practice relaxation and breathing techniques to control physical feelings of anxiety (see Chapter 3).
- Encourage the child to become more involved in group participation and to not draw special attention to himself by standing to the side or inappropriately reading a book during physical education class.
- Encourage the child to speak to others in class and help him respond to teasing.
- Speak to the physical education teacher about ways to change how teams are picked, such as a lottery system or having the student occasionally choose teams.

- Ask parents to practice a particular sport with a child so he is less self-conscious when playing the sport in class.
- Ask a child to be as prepared as possible with respect to his uniform and gear when entering the locker room.
- Ask the child to undress and prepare for class as quickly as possible and to actively speak to others while doing so to deflect worry about being watched or judged.

Extracurricular Activities

Admittedly, many kids attend school simply to interact with their friends and to network socially. This is fine as long as a child is in school and learning appropriately. If a child refuses to attend school, try to get him involved in various extracurricular activities at school. Go over a list of activities a child is eligible for and ask him to pick four or five he might consider attending. These activities could include academic, athletic, gaming, musical, or other central themes. Encourage the child to attend at least two extracurricular activities so, if one is dropped, another remains.

Active participation in extracurricular activities is helpful for several reasons. First, participation serves as practice for developing social skills, managing social anxiety, and developing friendships. Participation is especially helpful for youths in a racial minority, those with social anxiety, and those new to a school. Second, the activity may serve as a lure toward school attendance, especially if a child feels obligated to his group. Third, the development of friendships in these activities will likely increase the number of people a student knows in his daily classes. These friends can help buffer the child against anxiety and school-based threats such as teasing and can help monitor a child's attendance and encourage him to come to school if a day is missed. Finally, a child may wish to invite friends from a group for other activities outside of school.

Special Topics for Attention-Based Absenteeism

Other special circumstances tend to occur more among youths with attention-based absenteeism, and these are discussed here. All, however, could apply to youths who refuse school for other reasons.

Returning to School after a Break

A particularly difficult transition for many kids with school refusal behavior, especially those who did so for attention, is going back to school after some time off. This can apply to youths with current or past problems attending school. Suggestions for preventing relapse in a child with a past history of school refusal behavior are in Chapter 6. This section addresses youths with a current pattern of school refusal behavior.

If a child has been out of school because of a holiday or other scheduled break, parents should restart the regular morning routine at least a few days before school begins. This should involve rising times and morning preparation behaviors that mimic what would happen if a child were to attend school that day. Parents may even be encouraged in some cases to drive a child to school and wait several minutes before bringing her home. In this way, resuming school after some time off will not be so difficult. Parents can also plan a fun activity for the evening of the first day back to school and perhaps encourage a child to practice anxiety management techniques from Chapter 3. Most important, a child should be reminded of the necessity of attending school as well as consequences for not doing so.

Parents Missing Work to Attend School with a Child

Many kids who refuse school for attention insist that their parents attend school with them. Parents sometimes acquiesce to this demand just so a child goes to school. Parents thus serve as classroom volunteers or teacher assistants to be near their child and prevent morning misbehaviors. Unfortunately, parents miss work as a result or cannot extricate themselves from the school without triggering disruptive behavior from their child.

Obviously, parents should not miss work to attend school with their child. If a parent does find herself in this position, however, several strategies may be helpful. First, the parent should gradually withdraw herself from the child's classroom or school, perhaps about 15 minutes at a time. A parent who attends school with her child from 9:00–11:30 A.M., for example, can begin to leave at 11:15 A.M. Any subsequent behavior problems from the child should be met with classroom- and home-based consequences (see Chapter 4). If the child can handle the earlier departure time without disrupting the class, then the parent leaves 15 minutes earlier (i.e., 11:00 A.M.). This pattern can be repeated every 2–3 days or so until virtually no time is left.

Second, once a parent has successfully extricated herself from the classroom, she can establish a firm boundary that the child knows a parent will not cross. For example, parents may establish the main school lobby as a firm boundary. Whatever the child's future misbehavior, parents will go no further than the lobby. At this point, the child should be deposited with a school official who escorts the child to class. Misbehaviors should be met with home-based punishments that evening (see Chapter 4). Possible boundaries also include the school playground or library, main entrance, or other place outside the classroom depending on what is acceptable to parents and school officials.

Multiple Children Refusing School

Some families have multiple children who simultaneously refuse school. This commonly happens when one child refuses school, often to seek attention from parents, and models school refusal behavior for siblings. Of course, other functions may apply as well. In these cases, parents should first address the child *with the most severe school refusal behavior.* Successfully doing so often creates a "ripple effect" among siblings who model the return to school. In addition, ending the most severe case of school refusal behavior allows parents to have greater energy and determination for enhancing school attendance in other children. Cases such as this also require extensive social support. Bringing other adults into the morning situation to help get kids to school or escort a youth from class to class may be quite helpful.

Children with Developmental Disorders

Children with limited developmental disorders such as learning disabilities or more pervasive developmental disorders such as mental retardation or autism often refuse school as well. Most of these kids have an individualized education plan (IEP), so be sure to incorporate procedures to enhance school attendance into these plans. In addition, note that many procedures in this book likely require a *much slower pace* for kids with developmental disorders. Some techniques, such as cognitive procedures (Chapter 3), may not apply to this population at all. Many of these kids also become frustrated by schoolwork and are thus less motivated to attend school. Establishing some formal reward-based system for effort, modest academic gains, and attendance can be helpful for this population.

Special Topics for Tangibly Rewarded Absenteeism

Other circumstances may apply more to youths refusing school to pursue tangible rewards outside of school. These are discussed next but, again, could apply as well to any youth with school refusal behavior.

Calling the Police

Youths who leave a school campus during the day are obviously at risk for dangerous consequences. This includes youngsters who run away from an elementary school as well as middle and high school students who leave school during the day. In the case of a younger student who has left school during the day, contact the school or local police immediately. In addition, younger children known to be "flight risks" should be *escorted or otherwise supervised very closely during the school day to prevent such behavior.* Parents should obviously be notified immediately as well if a younger child has left school grounds. Ask parents to notify you if a child is not coming to school on a particular day so you do not wonder if the child fled school in the morning.

The situation is obviously a little different for teenagers who commonly leave school grounds. Although resources are limited, school officials or parents should contact police if a youth leaves school and might be engaging in dangerous or illegal behaviors such as drug use or joyriding. If possible, parents and school officials such as truant officers should also look for a child known to be out of school and bring him back. This is especially recommended if the student's whereabouts are known. A youth who knows he will be regularly tracked and returned to school is much less likely to leave school grounds than a youth who faces no consequences for such actions.

Motivating a Child

Some youths are admittedly difficult to motivate, and finding rewards for a contract can be quite challenging in certain cases. School-based rewards are sometimes more potent than home-based rewards, especially for youths with few privileges or resources at home. Examples include time spent with a certain teacher or counselor, computer privileges, assisting a librarian or custodian with his or her work, and exemptions for work-study programs. Parents may also have to be innovative about discovering home-based rewards for their children, so discuss with them even basic things such as computer or television time, types of food, discussions with friends, and more flexible bedtime as appropriate.

Problems Sleeping or Rising from Bed

Many teenagers who refuse school fall into poor sleeping habits. These youths may complain they cannot sleep and therefore cannot rise from bed on time in the morning. This problem may be due partly to normal physical changes that accompany adolescence and partly to parents who are lax about a child's bedtime and nighttime activities. Encourage youths and their parents to pursue a regimen of good sleep hygiene during the evening:

- The child should only *sleep* in her bed and not use it for reading, watching television, talking on the telephone, sending text messages, completing homework, or other arousing activities.
- The child should be in bed *with lights out* 8–9 hours before having to rise from bed.
- The child should avoid caffeine, nicotine, alcohol, and exercise before bedtime.
- The child should practice relaxation methods close to bedtime (see Chapter 3).
- The child should follow the same routine before bedtime and begin this routine 30 minutes before lights out.
- Parents should set a curfew for at least two hours before bedtime.
- Parents should speak to their pediatrician about sleep medication if necessary.

If a child has trouble rising from bed, encourage parents to rise early themselves and periodically wake the child prior to his rising time (essentially serving as a snooze alarm). Some parents prefer making loud noises as well to "motivate" a child to rise from bed. Contracts can also be designed to specifically target sleeping and rising behaviors. Parents should also understand that a child who rises late and fails to go to school on time must still attend school for whatever part of the day remains. It is better to have a child walk into school sleepily at 10:00 A.M. than miss the entire day.

504 and Individualized Education Plans

School districts are mandated to accommodate students with conditions that interfere with learning. Examples include medical problems and psychiatric conditions such as attention-deficit/hyperactivity or learning disorder (ADHD), depression, and anxiety. Special plans, such as 504 and individualized education plans (IEPs), allow you flexibility to address youths with school refusal behavior and psychiatric problems. These plans may be especially useful for establishing or modifying class schedules, makeup work, attendance regimens, and supervision and escorting practices. The plans should also be considered in cases when a child is at risk for failing a school year and has little incentive to return to school. In some cases, partial attendance and partial credit may still be possible and is preferable to abandoning a certain school year and trying anew in September.

Final Comments and What's Next

The chapters comprising this book so far have focused much on individuals and the "nuts and bolts" of what to do in specific cases of school refusal behavior. This trend continues in the first part of Chapter 6, which discusses ways of preventing relapse in a child with past school refusal behavior. However, the remainder of Chapter 6 and all of Chapter 7 cover more general strategies for addressing youths with school refusal behavior. In particular, these chapters cover systemic methods for this population as well as a discussion of contextual variables that impact school refusal behavior. Suggestions regarding these contextual variables are presented as well.

6

Preventive and Systemic Strategies for School Refusal Behavior

Sheen is a 9-year-old girl who recently completed fourth grade following episodes of school refusal behavior. In October, Sheen began refusing school due to general distress in the classroom that was not clearly linked to specific objects or situations. Sheen's parents allowed their daughter to remain home twice to try to quell her anxiety, but this seemed to make matters worse. By January, Sheen was missing 1–2 days of school per week and was enjoying the amenities of staying home. The school-based social worker, in conjunction with Sheen's parents, successfully reintegrated Sheen to her classroom setting on a full-time basis by the end of March. Sheen missed three days of school from the beginning of April to the end of the school year, but successfully passed fourth grade. Her parents, however, are concerned about a recurrence of their daughter's absentee problem when she starts fifth grade in the fall.

In cases like Sheen's, successfully reintegrating a child to school is not always the end of the story. Many kids with a history of school refusal behavior continue to show intermittent absentee problems in the future for various reasons. Some kids feel distressed about school at certain times, some encounter new anxiety-provoking social or evaluative situations, some test their parents' resolve about sending them to school, and some face more tempting offers from friends to miss school. In other cases, family members revert to old, dysfunctional ways once the absentee "crisis" has passed. This can lead again to lax supervision, inconsistent rewards and punishments, poor parent-school official relationships, and other problems that can produce relapse.

This chapter initially covers strategies for preventing relapse of school refusal behavior in children and adolescents. The chapter begins with a discussion of specific relapse prevention suggestions for school officials who address this population. Later in the chapter more general or systemic methods from the research literature to prevent school refusal behavior are discussed. The final part of the chapter covers large-scale, systemic methods to reduce problematic absenteeism overall. Suggestions are also provided for devising a triage system within your school to reduce problematic absenteeism based on methods described in this book.

Relapse Prevention for a Specific Child

For kids like Sheen, several strategies can be used to maintain gains you and parents have worked hard to achieve. These strategies can be used in cases involving slips as well as relapse. A *slip* represents some minor backsliding toward problematic school attendance, such as an occasional missed day, a temper tantrum before school on a Monday, or a spike in anxiety during an important test. Slips occur frequently, especially after breaks from school, and should not be given too much attention unless the problem worsens. Slips can usually be addressed quickly by practicing anew the strategies used to reintegrate a child to school with less distress (see Chapters 3–5).

Parents sometimes become discouraged when slips happen, thinking they are back to "square one." Let them know slips are common and that they must intensify their intervention efforts and remain in contact with you for the next few days. Encourage parents to be as independent as possible, however, so they can practice managing future slips without extensive help from you or other school officials.

Even so, slips can accumulate or intensify and possibly lead to relapse. *Relapse* represents more intense backsliding toward the original absentee problem. If Sheen experienced some distress when entering fifth grade but did attend her class, then this would be a slip. This slip could be addressed by reminding Sheen to practice her anxiety management techniques (see Chapter 3). If Sheen experienced some distress when entering fifth grade but the situation deteriorated so that she began missing several days of school, this may be a moderate relapse. Relapses can be moderate or severe, but in either case you want to actively prevent them. The following sections represent strategies for doing so.

Reminders Following Intervention

When a family successfully completes your intervention and a child returns to school with less distress, pat yourself on the back! Refer to the box for knowing when your intervention is finished. After you do so, however, *focus immediately on relapse prevention.* A good first strategy is to write down for family members a list of reminders or techniques most useful for helping the child return to school. In many cases you will find that three or four techniques were key to helping a child return to school. Examples include practicing proper breathing, using the STOP method to challenge and change unrealistic thoughts, establishing a set morning routine, administering appropriate rewards and punishments, and developing written contracts. In addition, intensely supervising a child's attendance and actively monitoring her anxiety level should continue to be staples for *all parents of this population.* Parents and children should keep this list of reminders and refer to it whenever a slip occurs.

Knowing When Your Intervention Is Finished

How do you know when your intervention is finished and you can start thinking about relapse prevention? In a sense, intervention and relapse prevention should never end because children and parents should continue practicing whatever techniques helped reintegrate a child to school. In addition, monitoring a child's attendance must continue over time. Still, one could ask when some of the more intensive intervention components could be lifted, such as escorting a child from class to class, maintaining attendance logs and strict supervision, and requiring parents to bring a child to your office.

My general recommendation is that a child be in school full-time for at least two weeks with a 75% reduction in ratings of distress before considering removal of these intensive components. Anxiety ratings around 8–9 on a 10-point scale, therefore, should now be around 2–3 (small amounts of manageable anxiety are fine). Even at this point, remove components of an intervention only gradually. Any slips on a child's part, especially immediate ones, should be addressed right away by reinstituting what worked before. In other cases, full-time school attendance was not the final goal. In these cases, I recommend continuing intervention until your final goal is reached, as opposed to some approximation of that goal. For example, if your final goal is to place a child in an alternative educational setting that requires five weekly hours of class time, then this is the minimum attendance to expect.

Practicing Techniques from the Intervention

Although many parents continue to practice techniques that helped their child return to school, others do not. Some parents naturally relax once an episode of school refusal behavior passes or they become preoccupied with other things. Other parents prematurely abandon an intervention when a child's attendance becomes minimally acceptable. This may be especially so for dismissive or confused parents (see Chapter 5). Parents who eventually become lackadaisical about your intervention or their child's attendance are at particular risk for slips and relapse.

Parents must understand that continued practice and vigilance from the end of intervention is the best way to prevent future problems. Parents should continue practicing techniques useful for returning a child to school, even during extended breaks from school if applicable. If parents have access to the "step one" self-directed book in this series (*Getting Your Child to Say "Yes" to School,* Oxford University Press), then they can periodically review sections most pertinent to them. *Parents should also vigilantly monitor their child's attendance and level of distress each day.* Parents must not take school attendance and low distress for granted, *especially in chronic cases of school refusal behavior.* In addition, parents should remain in close contact with you for several weeks or even months to ensure that their child remains in school and that related problems such as extensive makeup work are addressed.

Exploring and Addressing New Obstacles to School Attendance

A child's slip or relapse could be due to recent life changes instead of failure to practice certain techniques. Slips or relapse could follow recent traumas, child depression or other psychopathology, academic problems, class schedule or curricula changes, peer conflicts, or other new difficulties. Parents and at least one school official should have regular conversations with a child who recently refused school. The purpose of these conversations would be to explore and address new obstacles to attendance. Referrals to mental health professionals (see Chapter 1) may also be necessary.

Slips or relapse could also occur following a change in function of school refusal behavior. In other words, a child may find another reinforcer powerful enough to trigger absenteeism. In this case, reevaluate a child's function of school refusal behavior, perhaps using brief interview, school-based observation, and the School Refusal Assessment Scale-Revised (see Chapter 2). If a child now refuses school for a different function, then previous aspects of your intervention may not apply. For example, a child who initially refused school to avoid general distress but who now pursues tangible rewards outside of school will not benefit from more relaxation training.

Beginning of a New School Year

A child who previously refused school often has difficulty resuming school in the fall. This is particularly so if a child enters a school *for the first time,* especially middle school. Following are ideas to help a child integrate or reintegrate into school in the fall:

- Parents and the child should attend all scheduled orientation sessions held at the beginning of the school year.
- Parents should have all necessary school supplies purchased and ready at least one week before the start of school.
- Parents and child should go on a private tour of the school, with emphasis on the areas of transition most likely to be stressful for the child: school bus zones, gymnasium, art and music centers, cafeteria, library, playground, and your office and the main office.
- The child should know his bus schedule thoroughly as well as contingency plans in case he misses the bus. Parents can also have their child practice the routine of getting to the school bus in the morning and exiting the school bus to come home in the afternoon.
- Parents and the child should resume the regular school day morning routine 7–14 days before the beginning of school. This may even include a simulated bus ride to school so the child is familiar with stops and times.
- Parents should have a relaxed conversation with their child the night before school starts about concerns and potential obstacles to school attendance the next day.
- Parents should be flexible in their morning schedule the first day of school to address any jitters the child has about attending school or if he needs extra time to enter class.

Booster Sessions

Another relapse prevention method is *booster sessions,* or special meetings among you, parents, and a child who recently refused school. The purpose of booster sessions is to review skills and techniques from your intervention and discuss upcoming stressors that may interfere with school attendance. Booster sessions are often held during "high-risk" times such as immediately before the start of a new school year or during examination periods. In Sheen's case, her school-based social worker may wish to meet with Sheen and her parents before the start of fifth grade to boost skills needed to maintain her attendance. Booster sessions are especially important for kids moving from elementary to middle school and from middle to high school.

Reminders of a Child's Success

A relapse prevention method that can be fun is to have a child develop an art project that represents her gains during your intervention. A child like Sheen, for example, could collect photographs of herself engaging in difficult tasks such as entering school and class, talking to peers, speaking in front of her peers, and preparing for school in the morning. These photographs could be arranged in a mosaic or other project to illustrate her accomplishments and serve as a reminder of what to do in the future when she feels anxious. Videotapes, drawings, journals, storybooks, posters, and other creative methods of illustrating a child's successful return to school could also be used in this regard.

Structured Activities During a Break

Kids with a history of school refusal behavior can benefit from continued involvement in certain activities during breaks from school. Youths with a history of shyness and aversion to social and/or evaluative situations, for example, could participate in social groups, clubs, teams, or other organized activities during school breaks. They could also be expected to maintain contact with former classmates and current friends to arrange mutual play times, a fun night out, or dates. Youths with a history of attention-seeking behavior could engage in frequent activities involving independence from parents. Examples include sleepovers, day camp, and library programs. Youths with a history of pursuing tangible rewards outside of school could be required to maintain curfew, associate with proper friends, and finish chores to earn privileges. Parents should also maintain regular discipline with appropriate rewards and punishments during breaks.

Maintaining the Right Attitude

An important part of relapse prevention is parent attitude about regular school attendance. This means two things. First, parents should not allow backsliding. Once a child demonstrates he can attend school at a certain level, this is the minimum level parents should expect each day. If a child can attend school for only three hours a day, then this is the minimum to expect. Second, parents must maintain an attitude that only severe conditions (see Chapter 3) will allow a child to remain home from school. *The default option must always be to send a child to school, even if minor problems are present.* Parents must also bring a child to school at any time of the day rather than allow him to stay home or out of school for an entire day. Efforts on your part to help parents maintain a proper attitude about school attendance will serve to prevent relapse.

The strategies discussed so far in this chapter refer to a particular child with school refusal behavior. The next section covers general prevention strategies from the research literature that may provide you with additional suggestions for addressing cases of problematic absenteeism.

Systemic Prevention for One or More Children

Spencer is a 13-year-old boy who recently entered middle school. Although Spencer did fine socially and academically in elementary school, he has had great trouble adjusting to seventh grade. In particular, he feels overwhelmed by his number of new classes, teachers, homework, and peers. Spencer began complaining about school to his parents in September and displayed physical symptoms in October. Spencer has not yet missed a full day of school, though he has skipped five classes and often comes to the guidance counselor's office to talk. Overall, he seems sullen, withdrawn, and unmotivated. His parents and guidance counselor have grown increasingly worried about Spencer and whether he will begin to more actively refuse school.

Systemic prevention for our purposes refers to schoolwide or communitywide practices to help prevent problematic absenteeism. This section covers components of prevention practices applicable to a given school. These components may provide you with some additional ideas for reducing absenteeism or initial problems in a student such as Spencer or for several students at once.

Restructuring the Role of the Homeroom Teacher

One component of successful absenteeism prevention programs is to restructure the role of the homeroom teacher. This obviously applies more to middle and high school students and assumes that homeroom is required. However, elementary school teachers could be involved in this capacity as well, perhaps before the start of class. In essence, the role of the homeroom teacher is expanded from simple gathering and supervision of students in the morning to a broader role that may include the following:

- Identifying students such as Spencer who may be at risk for school refusal behavior.
- Providing students with detailed guidance regarding the school, such as class schedules and locations, special events such as a general assembly, and other circumstances pertinent to a given child, such as the need to attend the nurse's office for medication.
- Meeting briefly with high-risk students such as Spencer to review potential obstacles or problems during the day and how those obstacles/problems could be resolved.
- Maintaining close contact with parents to provide daily feedback about a child's performance and discuss expected problems.

In this model, the homeroom teacher acts as an immediate "touchstone" for information and problem resolution. This model may be especially helpful as students make the transition from one school building to another and especially from elementary to middle school. *The development of a monitoring and mentoring system for youths entering middle school is very important because this is a very stressful time for many of them.* In addition, the homeroom teacher could work closely with other officials, such as a school psychologist or school-based social worker, to help coordinate and implement interventions for youths with new school refusal behavior. Examples include helping a child practice relaxation techniques or cognitive strategies, providing rewards for attendance, escorting a child to his first-period class, and preparing attendance logs.

The homeroom teacher could also be a good source for assessment information (see Chapter 2). Examples include providing daily ratings of a child's anxiety, observing parent-child interactions, and briefly interviewing a child in the morning. Finally, the homeroom teacher can immediately note a certain child's absence from school that day and inform parents or other school officials. In this way, a child may be brought to school for at least part of the day rather than missing the entire day. Even in situations involving limited resources, the role of the homeroom teacher could at least include early identification and referral of students such as Spencer who are likely to begin missing substantial amounts of school.

Peers as Monitoring and Reinforcing Agents

In addition to the homeroom teacher, peers and classmates from a child's school can be enlisted to help prevent or reduce absenteeism. Peers chosen for this task are generally well liked or popular *and* willing to comply with adult requests regarding a prevention program. Students are generally more receptive to feedback from, and discussion with, popular peers because their own social status may be enhanced. In this model, peers or classmates are enlisted to do two main things.

First, peers are assigned to a targeted child such as Spencer who may be having difficulty attending school. When a targeted child is in school on a particular day, the assigned peer notes the attendance and provides social reinforcement. This obviously requires active participation by the assigned peer but utilizes a natural resource that does not tax school officials. When a targeted child is not in school on a particular day, the assigned peer contacts her at home that night to ask about the reason for nonattendance and encourage attendance for the next day. Attendance problems that begin to worsen can then be brought to the attention of you or another school official. In this way, a child's attendance and other problems are actively monitored but within a socially acceptable framework for many older students.

Second, peers may be assigned as youth advocates in situations in which a child transitions from another school or a correctional institution to a new school. In this scenario, the advocate assists a particular child with the transition and actively monitors attendance and related areas such as classroom behavior and grades. In other cases, the youth advocate is a school official, such as a guidance counselor, who supervises or works in tandem with the assigned peer. Transitional "teams" are thus established to monitor the progress of at-risk students and prevent serious attendance and academic problems as well as recidivism back to a correctional facility.

Maintaining a Student's Peer Group Across Homeroom and Classes

Some prevention programs have also focused on maintaining a child's peer group across homeroom and certain classes of the day. A particularly common program is to ensure that a child has several friends in his *homeroom and first three classes.* This helps increase motivation to attend school in the morning, ease anxiety about attending the entire day, and reduce attention-seeking behavior toward a parent. An alternative strategy is to ensure that a child's friends are present in classes at high risk for being skipped. A child may be more likely to attend difficult classes such as physical education or those involving performance before others if a solid support group is present.

Programs involving the homeroom teacher, assigned peers, and other student contact are partly designed to increase a student's attachment to people at school and her sense of obligation to attend. *It is important to develop some level of attachment to people in the school building among youths at risk for school refusal behavior.* Doing so may intersect as well with earlier recommendations that a child be involved in school-based extracurricular activities (see Chapter 5). A child who knows others are expecting him to attend school or even depending on him for some participation may be likely to attend school even if he is not particularly motivated otherwise on a given day.

Feedback to Parents with Token Economy

Another component of successful prevention is frequent feedback to parents within a systematic school-based incentive program. During the course of this book I have stressed the need to quickly and frequently inform parents of a child's status during an intervention. In this prevention model, the process is expanded so that parents are given daily information about a child's attendance, academic progress, homework, and classroom behavior. Ideally, this information is then linked to home-based rewards and punishments as appropriate.

A child's behavior within school can also be linked to a reward and punishment system that relies on incentive and response cost. A *token economy* is a system whereby a child receives tokens (for younger children) or points (for older children) for adaptive behavior that can be later exchanged for tangible rewards. Adaptive behaviors may include actual attendance, refraining from disruptive classroom or playground behavior, calling parents no more than once per day, completing attendance logs, and submitting finished homework. Token economies work best when a response cost component is added or when a child loses tokens/points for misbehavior. Youths should be fully informed about the rules and expectations of an established token economy. In addition, parents should be informed daily about a child's progress and token/point status.

School-based Rewards for Student Attendance and Related Behaviors

In addition to reward-based token economies, a key component of many successful prevention programs for absenteeism is systemwide recognition and reward for attendance and related behaviors such as academic progress or improved social skills. School officials sometimes focus so much on students with school refusal behavior that they neglect students who come to school even under adverse conditions. In addition, students with past school refusal behavior are sometimes neglected once their immediate absentee problem has passed.

Establishing a schoolwide system for recognizing and rewarding good attendance can be useful. In addition, this system should be implemented weekly as opposed to once per month, semester, or year. Youths with good attendance could be rewarded by having their names announced over the loudspeaker or at an assembly or by receiving certificates of appreciation or other tangible rewards for good attendance. In this way, a "culture" is established whereby students and parents understand that a particular school values attendance and monitors attendance frequently. Youths with past school refusal behavior could receive special recognition such as tokens for each week or month of successful attendance.

School-based Punishments for School Refusal Behavior

The flip side to school-based rewards for attendance is, of course, school-based punishments for school refusal behavior. Many school districts have specific policies to provide consequences to students who miss school. Unfortunately, these consequences are often unclear, unknown by many parents and teachers, or inconsistently applied. To help establish a culture whereby a school is known to value school attendance, frequent rewards as well as the *consistent application* of punishments is necessary. In addition, these consequences must be well known to parents and all relevant school officials.

Although resources may be limited, instances of school nonattendance should be addressed immediately. The most pertinent example is returning a child to classes as soon as he illegitimately leaves the school campus. In addition, I recommend punishments that *still permit a child to be in school.* Although counterintuitive, school districts commonly suspend a child from school for failure to attend. Instead, a focus could be on detentions, in-school suspension, school-based "service," and other methods that are onerous for a child and yet require him to be in school and complete academic work. Other common school or legal consequences of ongoing absenteeism include supervision by a probation officer, court appearances, fines, community service, suspending a student's driver's license, and deferring the date a student can first apply for a driver's license.

Parent and Child Support Groups

Another aspect of prevention regarding absenteeism is school-based support groups for parents or youths with existing or potential school refusal behavior. Support groups can include general skills training approaches to improve effective parenting. Examples include appropriate disciplinary strategies, parent commands, rewards for adaptive behavior, and resources for help in dire circumstances. More specific to school refusal behavior, parents could learn about anxiety management, parenting, and contracting strategies discussed in Chapters 3 and 4. Parents could also share contact information with group members to provide support to one another when a particular child refuses school. These groups can thus be one way to help a parent mobilize a social support network.

Child-based support groups for this population could focus on specific aspects of school refusal behavior or more general issues such as trauma. Youths who share anxiety about school, for example, could learn to manage their physical and cognitive symptoms together. Group members could also support one another and help monitor each other's attendance. Youths may also feel obligated to attend school simply to meet with fellow group members. Other programs involve general school-based support groups for youths who have experienced recent personal trauma as well as youths at risk for problems following schoolwide trauma such as a suicide, violent act, or natural disaster. In these groups, the focus is usually on appropriate venting of feelings, increased social interaction, grief counseling, and crisis management.

School-based support groups are commonly conducted by guidance counselors, school-based social workers, and school psychologists. However, youths often have special bonds with certain teachers who may be helpful members or facilitators of a group. You may also consider soliciting outside help from a community-based therapist experienced with issues such as anxiety or trauma management. Consultations with medical and other professionals may be instructive as well. School-based support groups could also be supplemented with home visits (see Chapters 5 and 7) to help reassure children and ease their transition back to school.

Educating Fellow Professionals About School Refusal Behavior

Another potentially important component of prevention for absenteeism is educating fellow school officials about school refusal behavior. Many school officials such as teachers work under misconceptions about students with school attendance difficulties and the various psychological and other problems experienced by this population. As a result, some teachers provide misinformation to parents, inappropriately insist that a particular child remain in school for an entire day, interfere with an established intervention, or fail to notice warning signs of future school refusal behavior in a student.

Educating fellow professionals at your school about the characteristics of youths with school refusal behavior is important. This could involve a professional development seminar, in-service training, handouts, listserve e-mail, or other widespread dissemination method. You may wish to summarize material from this book and other resources on school refusal behavior. In doing so, focus on common symptoms, the four main functions of school refusal behavior, the importance of daily assessment as well as various methods of assessment, and components of intervention and prevention. In addition, emphasize how teachers and other school officials can help identify youths potentially at risk for absenteeism as well as those already missing school (see Chapter 1 for symptoms associated with different functions). Teachers and other school officials should also know who to contact to initiate and coordinate services for these youths (the "point person" discussed in Chapter 5).

Teacher Support and Stress Reduction

When implementing a school-based program to reduce absenteeism, it is important to remember that many teachers are overburdened and have limited resources, including time. If you design a program that imposes substantially more work and time constraints on teachers and others, your program is not likely to succeed. To increase teacher support for the plan you wish to implement, whether for one student or schoolwide, try the following:

- Include pertinent teachers in the development of your intervention, seeking input about a child and what is and is not feasible, given limits on a teacher's time.
- Establish common planning periods for interventions, such as Mondays at 3:30 P.M. or each day at 11:55 A.M. for 10 minutes, so teachers can know to set aside and plan for a specific time to address a particular case or other cases of school refusal behavior in the future.
- Plan for these meetings in depth beforehand so the conversations are focused and everyone's role is clear.
- Frequently monitor and address the level of burden imposed on a given teacher following your proposed intervention.
- Consider methods of reducing teacher stress and recognizing and rewarding teachers for their contributions to your intervention and prevention plans.
- Occasionally monitor a teacher's practice of various intervention components and provide corrective feedback as necessary.
- Encourage teachers and other staff members to assume ownership and accountability for intervention and prevention plans.

Systemic Intervention for Many Youths

Ryleen is a school-based social worker at a large high school within several impoverished neighborhoods. She recently examined absenteeism statistics for her school for the past three years. On a daily basis, an average of 8.7% of students is completely absent. In addition, many students are late to school or miss one to two classes. Ryleen's discussions with parents and teenagers reveal widespread dissatisfaction with the school-based curriculum, frustration with school bureaucracy, poor motivation, and severe lack of resources. Discussions with teachers reveal widespread dissatisfaction with parent involvement, frustration with language and cultural differences, and oversized classroom populations. Although Ryleen has successfully resolved several cases of school refusal behavior, she wishes to investigate and perhaps implement more systemwide measures to reduce problematic absenteeism on a grander scale.

This chapter has thus far covered strategies that apply to one or several youths with school refusal behavior. In addition, the emphasis has been on prevention. The following sections summarize systemic or wide-ranging strategies to address many youths and reduce the overall prevalence of problematic absenteeism. Various components of these interventions are discussed, along with a triage model for this population. Please note that a comprehensive description of each of these approaches is beyond the scope of this book. This section provides an introduction to various systemic approaches for problematic absenteeism, but additional readings are provided in Appendix 2.

Self-contained Educational Units

One systemic approach to reduce problematic absenteeism and school dropout has been to restructure a traditional high school into smaller, self-contained educational units. This approach was developed in reaction to the enormous size and number of students in typical high schools. Educators in huge schools commonly lament that they cannot keep track of hundreds or thousands of youths. Many students refusing school or those who have other problems thus go unnoticed or do not receive appropriate or immediate services.

In a self-contained model, a limited number of students and teachers are assigned to independently spaced educational units. School-based social workers, school psychologists, and other specialists are also assigned to one or more units as appropriate and feasible. Within this model, one self-contained unit could include youths at risk for school refusal behavior. In this unit, youths with a history of problematic absenteeism could be closely monitored and actions could be taken quickly to reduce school refusal behavior. In smaller units, students can also come to know each other well and develop friendships. Close attachments to teachers and other school-based adults may be cultivated as well, especially if teachers can adopt an open-door policy for their students. Smaller or self-contained units also mean school officials within that unit can better maintain close contact with parents, meet regularly as a team to address budding problems such as absenteeism or academic decline, ensure kids attend their next class, and enhance school/unit safety.

Summer Bridge and Other Transitional Programs

Another important systemic approach to absenteeism involves programs to ease student transition to middle and high school. Many students such as Spencer have enormous difficulties simultaneously adapting to new peers and classes, increased homework, *and* developmental changes associated with adolescence. Onset of school refusal behavior is most common as kids enter middle school. In addition, a key predictor of school dropout is poor transition to high school.

Systemic programs to help ease the transitional process involve summer bridge projects as well as increased support as a child enters a new school. Summer bridge programs are often designed to reduce gaps in skills or academic credits youths may have as they enter middle and high school. If youths lag in reading or arithmetic skills, for example, assimilating into a more demanding academic setting can be quite problematic. Therefore, summer programs include extra tutoring, classes, or instructional time to address these gaps or help students recover academic credits. Following the start of school, extra academic activities may occur during evenings or Saturdays.

Another systemic method of easing transition is extra support as youths enter a new school. This extra support may involve a self-contained educational unit (see previous section), increased tracking of students' attendance and grades in key classes, extended teacher meetings to discuss individual student progress, and increased student-centered academic projects to boost motivation. Key academic classes such as reading or math can be repeated during a school day as well. Class periods and the role of the homeroom teacher (see earlier section) can also be expanded. Many of these programs also involve student support groups to address social skills deficits or develop academic skills such as organization and study skills. Teachers and other educators should be fully educated about aspects and warning signs for school refusal behavior. These transitional programs have been implemented successfully in many schools within impoverished areas.

Conflict Resolution

Conflict resolution among youths, parents, and school officials is another important systemic approach. Conflict resolution partly involves bullying and school violence (see Chapter 7). More common forms of school-based conflict that instigate nonattendance involve friction between youths, youths and their parents, and parents and school officials. Systemic conflict resolution for these dyads often consists of training sessions facilitated by school-based social workers or other specialized professionals.

Training sessions are usually held in a school setting and typically involve groups only for students and groups only for parents and school officials. Training sessions among students focus on developing better communication and problem-solving skills. Students may be asked to provide examples of peer conflict, discuss various responses to a conflict, role-play appropriate responses such as negotiation and de-escalation, increase empathy and tolerance for diversity, and appreciate another person's perspective. In addition, students must practice active listening, paraphrase others' statements, monitor nonverbal communication such as facial expressions, refrain from inflammatory statements such as insults or interruptions, and issue clear, appropriate statements themselves. Training sessions for adults involve learning to help students use these skills during school and practice the skills themselves when communicating with one another.

Increasing Parent-School Official Cooperation

In addition to reducing parent-school official conflict are systemic programs to increase cooperation between these parties. These programs are often helpful in settings in which teachers and parents come from highly divergent cultural backgrounds. Many teachers and other school officials are ill-informed about the family or cultural values of their students' parents. School officials may be unaware, for example, of a family's worry that a child's school attendance means rejection of traditional cultural values. Language barriers are obviously another obstacle to parent-school official cooperation.

In-service training programs are thus commonly used to educate school officials about diverse family and cultural values and styles, and to dispel stereotypes. Teachers may also be encouraged to listen carefully to the concerns of a given family, understand changing demographics within their geographical region, and pursue strategies to increase parent involvement in diverse families (see Chapter 7). School officials are also urged to collaborate with university professors, church groups, and other community organizations that are knowledgeable of, and intersect greatly with, diverse populations. Increasing diversity among teachers and other school officials is a primary recommendation within the research literature as well.

Customizing Curriculum and Instruction and Providing Mentors

Another systemic approach for problematic absenteeism and dropout is tailoring curriculum and instruction plans more closely to individual children's needs. One component of this approach is enhancing school climate (see Chapter 7). Another component is to develop a large system of alternative educational approaches such as vocational educational settings, alternative high schools, part-time instructional or partial credit programs, after school or summer courses, and credit-by-examination or equivalency diploma procedures.

Another primary component of this strategy is to assign all or at-risk youths to an advocate or mentor at the beginning of the school year. Mentors could be school officials or even advanced peers who track attendance and academic progress. In addition, a mentor is responsible for helping youths develop an academic schedule that meets their credit requirements and sufficiently increases their motivation to attend school. The mentor is responsible as well for educating youths about long-term plans for college and for helping youths tailor their curriculum toward that goal.

Another key expectation of mentors is to link students to voluntary school-based mental health services as necessary and appropriate. On a systemic level, all youths and their families could be screened for psychological and other problems that interfere with school attendance. A more limited approach focuses on at-risk youths, perhaps those with a history of school refusal behavior. Mental health services could involve community-based professionals who devote time to developing student skills and social and academic competence as well as reducing symptoms of major mental disorders. In broader cases, mentors can link families to social service agencies to boost financial, housing, employment, and other tangible support.

Early Education, Family, and Health Services

Other researchers have focused on systemic programs to provide early education, family, and health services to impoverished families. These programs can extend from preschool to third grade and focus academically on early language and math skill development, structured small group learning experiences, full-day kindergarten, and low student-to-teacher ratios. More broadly, these programs include family outreach activities such as mobilizing resources, providing home visits, and enrolling children in school. Parents are also encouraged and given support to complete high school themselves, volunteering in their child's classroom, and participating in school-based events such as assemblies and field trips. Health services include screening for medical and other disorders, enhancing nutrition, and providing speech, nursing, and meal assistance. These programs have been shown to reduce overall school dropout rates.

Court Referral and Community Services

Other systemic approaches for problematic absenteeism involve community services partnered with the legal system. In many cases, some revision is made to the traditional court process for youths with extended school refusal behavior. One such revision involves placing court proceedings within certain school buildings to reduce transportation and stigma problems associated with attending a traditional courtroom. In addition, caseworkers from various community agencies serve as advocates or facilitators by linking family members to necessary and available resources, supposedly to ease parents' financial and other burdens so they can focus more on a child's school attendance. This approach is akin to the "one-stop shopping" model discussed in Chapter 5 that coordinates various services and meetings for families in one place: the school.

A similar model that revises the regular courtroom process is an informal program to help divert youths from extended school refusal behavior. One goal of this model is to help youths avoid having a legal record as a status offender. Following home visits and other assessments, a case management plan is established for each youth and his family. This plan may consist of reducing obstacles to attendance, such as providing transportation to school. The plan could also include assigned mentors, increased monitoring of attendance, parenting classes, social skills and anger management training, academic tutoring, and referrals to social service and community agencies.

In a related model, a school attendance officer monitors excessive absences and visits a family's home if necessary to provide information about available social service and community agencies. Issues that prevent good school attendance are also addressed if feasible. Ongoing attendance problems are then referred to a traditional court process. In a twist of this model, regular police officers identify and detain youths with excessive absences and refer them to a pre-established community center. The community center is designed specifically for youths with extended absences and provides services to address reasons for ongoing school refusal behavior. These models have been generally successful for reducing numbers of unexcused absences.

Police Pick-up and Return to School

Another systemic model for problematic absenteeism is a special police unit that recovers absentee adolescents and returns them to school. Parents are contacted as well. Youths may be referred to the traditional legal process for extended absences but can also be assigned to a special administrative unit with a school. This unit is essentially an in-school suspension program that focuses on intense supervision, completion of academic work, and remediation of obstacles to regular attendance. Programs such as these, though successful, depend heavily on parent involvement and use of community-based resources to maintain attendance gains.

Triage Model

You can see from this book that many ideas and programs exist for reducing school refusal behavior. Key questions facing many school officials, therefore, are how to utilize limited resources to implement all of these good ideas and which ideas are most appropriate for which students. One method is to consider the functional model of school refusal behavior presented in this book to address the unique characteristics of a given case and improve outcome rates. In addition, I recommend a "triage" model for school officials with many cases of problematic absenteeism at their school.

A triage model divides youths with school refusal behavior into various levels of absenteeism based on severity and chronicity of symptoms and additional problems. Resources such as number of school officials, time, and consultations with outside agencies are appropriated according to the intensity of school refusal behavior cases. As such, you must consider available resources at your school as well as administrative support when developing a triage plan. What follows here is a general blueprint of one basic triage model, but note that additional levels could be constructed.

The lowest level of a triage plan for problematic absenteeism, or *yellow level* to indicate warning, might include students who are just beginning to refuse school and have few additional learning, psychological, or family problems. These youths may have difficulty transitioning from one school to another, display general or social school-based distress for the first time, or demonstrate increased attention-seeking behavior. Interventions for these youths may include those less taxing for school officials. Examples include use of peer mentors, increased supervision, and classroom-based consequences for inappropriate behavior. Parents may also be referred to the "step one" self-directed book for school refusal behavior that is part of this series (see Chapter 1).

An intermediate level of problematic absenteeism, or *orange level* to indicate intensified problems, might include students with extended or moderate episodes of school refusal behavior and perhaps some learning, psychological, or family problems. These youths may be refusing school after some period of good attendance or were once in the "yellow" level but now have more sizable problems. They may be missing several classes or days of school, show substantial anxiety about school, or display worsened morning misbehaviors to stay home. Interventions for these youths may necessarily include at least one school official who can supervise a given case and provide an appropriate response. Consultation with other educational professionals is likely, and consultation with mental health and medical professionals is potentially necessary. Interventions discussed in Chapters 3–5 are those most appropriate for this intermediate, moderate level of school refusal behavior.

The highest level, or *red level* to indicate the most severe problematic absenteeism, might include students who persistently miss school or otherwise have trouble attending classes for extended periods of time. In addition, these students may have intense learning, psychological, or family problems. Some of these students were perhaps once at the "orange" level but now have very serious school refusal behavior that likely interferes with academic performance. In addition, some may have severe comorbid problems such as attention-deficit/hyperactivity or learning disorders. Other youths in this category have moderate school refusal behavior but also extremely difficult parents, dysfunctional families, or impoverished conditions.

Interventions for these youths will likely have to involve a "team" approach that includes different school officials. The team would meet regularly to discuss youths in the "red" level, design individualized educational and 504 plans for these youths, and maximize supervision for certain kids. Interventions for these youths may require a blend of individual and systemic interventions described in this book. In addition, interventions at this level should include referrals to appropriate legal, mental health, and social service agencies and consultations with clinical child psychologists and psychiatrists.

You and your fellow educational professionals may wish to develop a triage system at your school to address youths with various levels of school refusal behavior. A common fault in school districts is having an unclear plan to address problematic absenteeism or imposing all absentee problems onto one or two people. Instead, it is much more effective to take a structured team approach that includes parents, the child, school-based social workers, guidance counselors, school psychologist, principal or dean, relevant teachers, school nurse, and other educational professionals. One school-based official could serve as the "chair" or "point person" for this team, and the chair could be rotated periodically to ease stress. Such a team must remove obstacles to school attendance, work closely with parents, and implement techniques described in this book.

Final Comments and What's Next

This chapter covered relapse and general prevention as well as systemic interventions for youths with school refusal behavior. Some of these systemic interventions intersect with programs to address general problems associated with school refusal behavior—examples include bullying, violence, and lack of parent involvement. The next chapter covers contextual variables associated with school refusal behavior and provides suggestions for addressing these variables.

7

Contextual Variables and School Refusal Behavior

Joaquin is a 15-year-old boy in tenth grade who has missed several days of school this year and is considering dropping out of his large, urban high school. Joaquin says he is bored with school and that teachers are more concerned with rules than education. He has no long-term plans but has received two offers to work in his neighborhood. Joaquin seems disenchanted with school in general and figures he can drop out and complete his GED test at some future time. His parents seem relatively unconcerned about their son's decision process in this regard.

Serena is a 16-year-old girl in eleventh grade who has begun to skip school regularly after lunch. Her grades over the past four months have declined to the point that Serena believes it is pointless to return to school. Her parents are frustrated with their daughter's behavior and have told her she must find a job if she is not going to attend school. The option of finding a job is tempting for Serena because she feels alienated from peers and teachers at school. She has also thought of starting a family of her own.

Joaquin and Serena represent cases of absenteeism clearly influenced by factors broader than the psychological ones emphasized in earlier chapters. In these cases, economic, social, academic, and other environmental factors affect school attendance. Chapter 1 provided a brief summary of contextual variables that surround school refusal behavior and school dropout. This chapter takes a more detailed look at these broader variables and outlines some strategies to consider when addressing these complex cases. This chapter begins with specific predictors of school refusal behavior and dropout and proceeds later with a discussion of more general contextual variables.

Specific Predictors of School Refusal Behavior and Dropout

Why do youths refuse to go to school? The answer to this question lies partly in the functions of school refusal behavior emphasized in earlier chapters. Youths often refuse school to avoid school-based distress, escape from aversive social or evaluative situations, pursue attention from significant others, and pursue tangible rewards outside of school. When youths are asked why they missed school on a particular day, however, they sometimes provide less technical answers. Many youths say they missed school because they missed the school bus, felt sick or generally unmotivated to attend, overslept, or had no way of getting to school. In addition, many cannot develop a reason for missing school on a certain day.

Why do youths drop out of school? When sophomores who prematurely left school are asked this question, their answers are varied and summarized in Table 7.1. Their answers generally surround themes such as having been out of school for some time, academic and peer problems, dislike of school and its curriculum, and economic pressures. Several of the reasons Joaquin and Serena were considering school dropout are on this list, including pursuit of work, GED test, and desire to start a family.

Another way of knowing why youths refuse or drop out of school is to examine specific predictors of problematic absenteeism. Researchers have identified many predictors of school refusal behavior and dropout, and these can be generally divided into community, school, parent/family, and child predictors (see Appendix 2 for pertinent references). Some predictors overlap with adolescent self-reports mentioned earlier.

Community-based predictors of problematic absenteeism include disorganized or impoverished neighborhoods, especially neighborhoods with strong gang-related activity and interracial tensions. Poor social support, inadequate child supervision, and lack of services to address problematic absenteeism may be endemic in these neighborhoods as well. Youths who live in areas where substantial economic

Table 7.1 Percentage of High School Sophomores Who Left School Prematurely by Reason

Reason for Leaving School	Percentage
Missed too many school days	43.5
Thought it would be easier to get GED	40.5
Getting poor grades/failing school	38.0
Did not like school	36.6
Could not keep up with schoolwork	32.1
Became pregnant	27.8
Got a job	27.8
Thought could not complete course requirements	25.6
Could not get along with teachers	25.0
Could not work and go to school at same time	21.7
Had to support family	20.0
Did not feel belonged there	19.9
Could not get along with other students	18.7
Was suspended from school	16.9
Had to care for a member of family	15.5
Became father/mother of a baby	14.4
Had changed schools and did not like new one	11.2
Thought would fail competency test	10.5
Did not feel safe	10.0
Was expelled from school	9.9
Got married/planned to get married	6.8

Source: National Center for Education Statistics (2006).

lures exist, such as plentiful jobs that require little education, may also be at risk for problematic absenteeism.

Major *school-based predictors* of problematic absenteeism are listed in Table 7.2. Many of these variables contribute to a poor school climate and indifference or neglect of a child's individual educational needs and absenteeism. Factors that contribute to poor student attachments with peers and teachers are important as well. Examples include

Table 7.2 School-based Predictors of School Refusal
Behavior and Dropout

Corporal punishment

Curriculum irrelevant to a student's needs

Decreased homework and teaching time

Discrepancies between a student's ability and performance

Ethnic/racial differences

Frequent student and teacher absences

Frequent changes of schools and service placements

Inadequate documentation of absences/poor monitoring of attendance

Inappropriate retention or promotion of a student

Inappropriate school placements, as for students with learning disorders

Inconsistent enforcement of rules regarding absenteeism

Lack of educational goals for students

Lack of praise for student achievement

Low expectations for student achievement

Perceived discontinuity between current classes and later life experiences

Poor teacher competence

School transitions

School violence and class disruptions

Unwillingness of school officials to work with family members or
outside professionals

Use of suspensions and expulsions to discipline students with
excessive absences

ethnic/racial dissonance, teacher absences, frequent changes of school placements, use of suspensions as a disciplinary tool, and school violence. Systemic strategies to improve school climate (see later section) are likely necessary to address school-based predictors of problematic absenteeism.

Major *parent/family-based predictors* of problematic absenteeism are listed in Table 7.3. These predictors can be generally sorted into three categories. The first category is difficult parents and problematic family dynamics (see Chapter 5 for more detail) related to poor

Table 7.3 Parent/family-based Predictors of School Refusal Behavior and Dropout

Child maltreatment

Family transitions such as divorce, illness, unemployment, or moving

Few study aids at home

Inadequate parent supervision

Lack of social or financial support

Large families (5+ children)

Low parent expectations regarding attendance and education

Low parent knowledge, motivation, or interest regarding absenteeism

Poor communication with school officials

Poor parenting skills

Problematic family dynamics

School dropout among relatives

Single-parent families

Stressful home life

supervision and parenting skills, and low motivation to resolve absenteeism. The second category is lack of resources with respect to social support, finances, time, and academic aids at home. The third category is intense family stress possibly caused by transitions in employment, housing, health, and marital status. Cultural differences and inability to speak English may be important predictors of absenteeism as well. Strategies to increase parent involvement are discussed later in this chapter.

Major *child-based predictors* of problematic absenteeism are listed in Table 7.4. Child-based predictors are quite varied and do not fall neatly into specific categories. In general, however, poor academic and social competencies are key to children's behavior problems, including absenteeism. Associations with deviant peers, poor long-term outlook regarding education, emotional and behavioral disorders, history of absenteeism and dropout, trauma, and work outside of school are powerful predictors of school refusal behavior and dropout. For many kids with these characteristics, school-based programs to boost social

Table 7.4 Child Predictors of School Refusal Behavior and Dropout

Alienation from school

Association with deviant peers or those who have dropped out of school

Being 2+ years older than one's school peer group

Discrepancy between grade level and reading level

Disruptive behavior

Dissatisfaction with or lack of enjoyment at school

Emotional trauma

Emphasis on immediate gratification or de-
 emphasis on a long-term educational strategy

Extensive work hours outside of school

Fear of competition

History of poor grades or retention in one or more grades

Intolerance of structured activities

Lack of social skills, intense social/evaluative anxiety,
 or feelings of unpopularity

Poor health or self-esteem

Poor proficiency in English or math

Poor relationships with authority figures

Poor commitment to school or educational goals

Poor student participation in extracurricular activities

Previous dropout

Psychopathological or cognitive problems

and academic competencies and mental health interventions to reduce symptoms of mental disorder are likely imperative.

 These specific predictors are sometimes part of more general contextual variables that surround school refusal behavior. A complete, comprehensive discussion of all contextual variables for school refusal behavior and dropout is beyond the scope of this chapter. However, a summary of these contextual variables and recommendations for school-based professionals are presented next. Pertinent references to support this discussion are in Appendix 2.

Contextual Variables

Recall from Chapter 1 that contextual variables are broad environmental events that indirectly affect a child's behavior. Several of these events were introduced in Chapter 1 and alluded to throughout the course of this book. The sections that follow return to these topics with some suggestions for school-based professionals.

Homelessness and Poverty

Homelessness and poverty are obviously significant barriers to school attendance for many children. As a school official, you may not be able to tackle homelessness and poverty on a grand scale but you can consider some things for an individual case. For a child whose family is homeless, for example, consider ways of helping parents waive or meet requirements for enrollment. Explore creative ways of having a child attend school even if parents have difficulty finding or providing necessary documentation. This might involve allowing the child to attend the school library and complete academic work without yet attending classes. You are obviously bound to certain legal statutes regarding undocumented students. If you know a child will eventually qualify for school, however, facilitating this process in whatever way possible will greatly enhance the child's chances for learning, obtaining academic credits, passing the grade, and developing friendships.

Systemic strategies for impoverished families were discussed in Chapter 6. For individual cases of impoverished students, linking parents to social service, mental health, legal, and other community agencies will likely be necessary. Increasing financial and other support for a family may also lessen pressure on an adolescent to prematurely leave school to work. Consider as well coordinating family appointments with various agencies at your school to reduce transportation and other logistical problems that can lead to missed meetings and noncompliance.

Teenage Pregnancy

Teenage pregnancy is a serious risk factor for premature departure from school. Many adolescent girls (and some boys) leave school during late stages of their pregnancy or immediately after the child is born. Some researchers wishing to address this issue have designed *school-based health centers* that allow pregnant females to access prenatal and postnatal care without missing classes. These centers provide medical and nutritional health care, which in many cases may be the only care a mother receives during and after her pregnancy. Some school-based health centers have been expanded as well to include mental health care and linkages to social services for family members. The success of school-based health centers relies on their convenience for students who can stay on a school campus for medical appointments. These centers have been shown to lower rates of absenteeism during the prenatal period and increase attendance at an alternative school during the postnatal period.

You may not be able to establish a wide-ranging health center at your school, but consider ways of enhancing attendance for individual pregnant teens. In doing so, you may wish to consult with your school nurse or other available school-based medical professionals. One suggestion would be to facilitate a teenager's medical appointments at your school so fewer classes are missed. This may not be possible for elaborate needs such as ultrasound testing but may be more feasible for generic needs such as nutritional and parenting education, daily monitoring, and minor medical issues. Mental health services could be provided within the school setting as well. Another suggestion is to prearrange placement in an alternative educational setting that allows a teenager to care for her new baby and yet continue to secure academic credits.

School Violence and Victimization

School violence and victimization are key contextual variables linked closely to school absenteeism and dropout. For this discussion, separate sections are provided for the broader problem of school violence and then the more specific problem of bullying.

School Violence

School violence represents a systemwide problem that creates an atmosphere of intimidation and threat for students, teachers, and others. Programs to reduce school violence have focused on intervention as well as prevention. Intervention approaches include crisis management and victim assistance following a violent episode, counseling services to address subsequent emotional disorders and racial conflicts, and parent and family counseling to reduce child maltreatment. Many schools also provide conflict resolution methods, skills training groups for aggressive and victimized children, and extracurricular activities to reduce tension.

Administrators often suspend, expel, or transfer violent or potentially violent students, such as those who bring a weapon to school. Teachers may receive training about mediating peer disputes, classroom management, safety practices during a violent episode, and curricula to boost social and academic competencies. Broader approaches include increased security via metal detectors, surveillance cameras, guards, locker searches, closed campuses, restricted entryways, dress codes, and enhanced lighting. Linkages to community based youth and church groups and police and anti-gang programs are also common in violence-prone schools.

Prevention programs have also been developed for systemic school violence. One systemic approach is skills development, especially with respect to impulse and anger control, interpersonal negotiation and problem solving, and understanding emotions. Another approach is to monitor warning signs of violent activity in individual students, including sudden isolation or disengagement, impulsivity, substance use, and threats or actual physical aggression. Students identified as at risk can be referred to mental health services. Other prevention programs reach outside the school campus to include home visits. These visits are designed to improve parenting skills, management of aggressive behavior, and student academic performance. Peer-based programs have been developed as well to curb school violence but have not been found to be particularly effective.

Bullying

School violence has also been examined in more specific instances such as bullying. Victims of bullying are clearly less likely to attend school, especially if previous instances of victimization have occurred. Several school-based approaches have been designed to reduce overall bullying rates. One school-based approach involves curricula changes or educating children about bullying and modifying course content to emphasize cooperative group work and social problem-solving skills. Other schoolwide programs to reduce bullying include group training interventions to develop social skills in bullies and increasing the number of school officials who focus on bullying episodes. Unfortunately, these programs have produced only mixed results.

Other systemic approaches are more effective for reducing bullying. A multidisciplinary or "whole-school" approach, for example, involves developing a consistent schoolwide model to address bullying. The model is developed for an individual school by a large team of teachers, school-based mental health professionals, administrators, and parents and students. In this way, everyone at the school becomes more aware of bullying and commits to implementing the plan during and following its construction. The plan generally involves removing positive consequences for bullying, such as attention or tangible rewards, and increasing negative consequences such as detention or suspension. *Instances of verbal and physical aggression are also clearly defined, and rules and consequences regarding such aggression are widely disseminated.* Students, teachers, and parents are then expected to assiduously monitor, report, or address instances of bullying.

Whole-school programs are effective for reducing overall rates of bullying. These programs may be supplemented by other systemic ideas such as conflict resolution or mediation programs for students and student tribunals that sanction bullies for specific infractions. Improved supervision during quasi-school or non-classroom interactions, such as on playgrounds and before and after school, is recommended as well. Reparations from a bully to a victim may be appropriate in some cases. Anonymous surveys of students and teachers regarding the nature and prevalence of bullying can accompany whole-school approaches to evaluate their effectiveness.

You may be more likely to see an individual child who suffers from effects of bullying and who thus refuses school. For an individual case, carefully evaluate whether a bullying incident or threat has actually occurred because some youths exaggerate perceived threats to avoid school. If a real threat is plausible, then some intervention is necessary to protect the safety of the student and address the perpetrator according to school and legal policy. A key problem in many school districts is that bullying is not consistently addressed or punished. Bullies must know that negative consequences will certainly follow threatening acts.

Inform parents of the victim and bully about the situation and your subsequent actions. If possible, also increase supervision of the victim and bully during the school day. This monitoring will likely have to continue for some time, perhaps months. In addition, encourage victims to travel the campus with friends or others, avoid isolated situations, demonstrate appropriate assertiveness, and quickly report instances of bullying or threat to a school official. Some youths will also need help reducing self-blame for bullying. If a child feels socially isolated at school, then providing him with a peer mentor may be helpful. The peer mentor could help the child traverse school hallways, provide feedback about various social and threatening situations, and serve as a contact for information about a bullying episode.

Encourage youths to ignore taunts and threats as much as possible, especially youths who are not particularly socially skilled. In this regard, also recommend role play and other strategies to develop social skills in victimized children. Note as well that some parents recommend retaliatory violence to reduce bullying, but this strategy is not plausible for many youths. In more substantial or chronic cases, removal of the bully from the school campus may be necessary.

In more manageable cases, helping a bully enhance negotiation and social skills, problem-solving and listening abilities, positive self-concept, impulse and anger control, and empathy toward others is recommended. Empathy training can involve recognizing that others have different perspectives, taking the perspective of others, taking responsibility for one's actions, identifying emotions in oneself and others, and tutoring victims of bullying. In general, greater emotional connection is sought between a perpetrator and a victim. However, perpetrators should also have a clear understanding of punishments for their actions.

Some youths refuse school when bullied, which is understandable. However, some youths continue to refuse school even after a legitimate threat is removed or otherwise neutralized. Ongoing refusal to attend school in these cases may be due to residual fear of harm, maladaptive thoughts, attention seeking, desire to remain home, or other reasons. School refusal behavior that follows elimination of a threat and thus is no longer justified must be addressed as you would for a child who never faced a threat. The techniques discussed in earlier chapters would apply at this time, though sensitivity to a child's concerns about future threat is fine. The expectation that the child must attend school, however, should not change in this situation.

School Climate

School safety issues are an important part of the broader concept of school climate. School climate generally refers to student feelings of connectedness to their school and the degree of support a student feels for academic and other needs. Recall from Chapter 1 that poor school climate is closely related to student boredom as well as problematic absenteeism and school dropout. Poor school climate was a key reason Joaquin and Serena, the cases presented at the start of the chapter, considered leaving school.

School safety is obviously an important aspect of school climate, but other factors are involved as well. School climate seems intricately related to high teacher morale, positive and constructive communication between faculty and administrators, and high academic and behavioral expectations for students. Good climate is also related to orderly classrooms, high student activity in extracurricular activities, low racial tension, schoolwide traditions and ceremonies, similar codes of conduct for students and school officials, adherence to *clearly stated* rules, and consistent and fair treatment of students. In related fashion, disciplinary practices are not automatic or necessarily harsh, and school rules are not robotically cited. Instead, student infractions are considered on a case-by-case basis, and consequences are graded and administered after careful consideration of mitigating factors and student history.

The variable perhaps related most to good school climate is closely matching curricula and educational programs to a student's unique academic needs and interests. This can mean several things, including flexible course scheduling, electives, tutoring, matching course content to a child's cognitive ability and interests, modifying course content often to keep it interesting, and developing educational plans that consider each child's strengths and limitations. Frequent reevaluations of a child's academic status and appropriate placement within school are important as well. *This is especially important for youths with learning problems who may be at special risk for school refusal behavior* (see Chapter 1).

Matching curricula to a student's academic needs and interests also requires ongoing feedback from a student about her coursework and long-range plans. Frequent student-teacher (or other school official) contact is thus crucial. This contact can also involve building a child's internal locus of control so the student assumes more responsibility and accountability for her academic status. Charting a child's success at school and providing regular rewards for school achievement are thus necessary. In addition to internal locus of control, researchers have found that developing a child's sense of hope about prospects for his future, including college attendance and occupational advancement, is a good buffer against school dropout.

All of these methods to increase positive school climate are designed to increase a child's sense of connectedness or attachment to his school and reduce social alienation. In this way, a child feels a greater sense of obligation and motivation to attend school, feels less bored, and decreases his dislike of school (see also Chapter 5). This sense of connectedness should translate into reduced absenteeism and reduced chance of dropout. Increased connectedness to school may also reduce ancillary problems such as associations with deviant peers, drug use, delinquent activity, and violence.

Parent Involvement

A particularly frustrating problem faced by school-based professionals is poor parent involvement in a child's education or attendance. Recall that Joaquin's parents were not especially involved in his academic process, which may have led partly to his disenchantment with school. Parent involvement refers to such things as attending parent-teacher conferences, checking homework, engaging in reading with the child, limiting television, becoming active in the development of a child's school, and monitoring school attendance. Lack of parent involvement may be due to several reasons, including parent/family- and school-based issues.

Parent-based reasons for poor parent involvement include belligerence, dismissiveness, and confusion (see Chapter 5). Another parent-based reason for poor involvement is a belief that responsibility for a child's education lies more with school officials than parents. This belief may intersect with *poor self-efficacy*, or a parent's view that he or she is not competent enough to help a child with homework or communicate effectively with school officials. Parents may also feel they cannot decipher their child's report cards or progress reports or feel embarrassed about sending notes to teachers that are full of spelling and grammatical errors.

Poor parent involvement also intersects with child temperament. Parents of a child with little interest in school activities and substantial defiance, for example, may become more disinterested in their child's education than parents of a more academically motivated child.

This applies more to adolescents than children and may reflect parent frustration with a teenager, history of contentious meetings with school officials about a child's misbehavior, and increased complexity of homework in high school. Parents also tend to be less involved with sons than daughters.

Family members with intense stressors, poor social support, or very few resources may also be less likely to monitor a child's educational needs and attendance. Single parents and parents who do not speak English are generally less involved in a child's educational activities as well. Parent concern about immigration status and potentially negative consequences of interacting with school officials must be considered. Increased family size, child care obligations, and transportation problems are other obstacles to parent involvement.

Broader school-related factors also pertain to poor parent involvement. Poor quantity and quality of parent-school official communication, as well as negative attitudes toward partnering with minority and low-income parents, are clearly related to parent withdrawal. Teachers and other school officials may believe that communication with certain parents is pointless or overly difficult, especially when language barriers are present. This may translate into fewer teacher requests to parents to become involved in classroom activities. Other school-based factors include cultural differences between parents and school officials, teacher absenteeism and inexperience, larger and more bureaucratically oriented schools (especially high schools), low expectations of students, and relaxed attitudes about academic achievement. School-based factors contributing to poor parent involvement tend to affect boys more than girls.

How can one improve parent involvement? Most researchers claim that in-home communication and education with parents is important. This may involve home visits to inform parents about their child's academic status, teach parents how to tutor their children (or learn themselves about their child's material), schedule regular parent-school official communications, and invite parents to the classroom. This may be a good opportunity as well to train parents to monitor their child's attendance, report absences quickly to a particular school official, and develop and implement interventions to reintegrate a child to school with less distress. If resources are limited, focusing on at-risk youths with substantial attendance or academic problems may be considered.

Researchers have also focused on ethnic differences regarding parent involvement. A key problem is that teachers often have little training about divergent family lifestyles, cultural backgrounds, and values that characterize many of their students. This can lead to inappropriate academic practices based on stereotype or traditional European-American culture. Researchers thus recommend schoolwide assessment of curricula as well as in-service training to educate teachers about changing demographics within their school and cultural lifestyles and values of their students' families. Another suggestion is to establish parent resource centers within schools that include interpreters to boost communication with teachers and recruit diverse parents to serve in parent-teacher associations and governing positions.

Broader suggestions for improving parent involvement include modifying a school environment toward smaller educational units and providing summer bridge and transitional programs that require parent input (see Chapter 6). School administrators can also try to better match the ethnicity of school personnel to the local community. As mentioned in Chapter 6, consulting with community members active within local diverse institutions such as social clubs, activity centers, and churches can also be useful to encourage greater parent involvement in education.

Medical Problems

Another contextual variable closely associated with school absenteeism is widespread medical problems among students. Recall from Chapter 1 that a leading cause of absenteeism worldwide is asthma and other respiratory illnesses. In addition, many children miss school during winter because of cold and flu symptoms. Researchers have examined schoolwide programs to reduce these symptoms and boost attendance rates. One set of school-based programs has focused on managing asthma symptoms in these ways:

- Educating parents and children about asthma symptoms.
- Ensuring that children use medications and peak flow meters appropriately.
- Increasing a child's physical strength.
- Maintaining contact with a physician.
- Monitoring daily symptoms.
- Providing access to a full-time school nurse.
- Reducing indoor pollutants.

Consistent school responses to asthmatic attacks should be instituted as well, but these responses should focus partly on methods to *maintain a child's attendance* on a particular day. In other words, a set policy of always sending home a child following asthma symptoms should be avoided.

Other schoolwide programs to boost student health include comprehensive hand-washing practices, use of hand sanitizers, mass flu immunization, and lice management. Most schools also have policies for addressing youths with severe or chronic medical problems, which often include an individualized education plan. Researchers of pediatric populations commonly recommend that these youths maintain home and school routines as regularly as possible. I recommend pursuing strategies that allow a child with a medical condition to attend school and interact with friends as much as possible. Home schooling or home-based instruction need not be the automatic response for these children.

Final Comments

I hope you find this book helpful for addressing many cases of school refusal behavior you face each day. Having interacted with this population for many years, I know how time-consuming, intense, and personally frustrating many of these cases can be. *Please remember the work you do on these cases is extremely important!* You may find little reward or praise from others when you successfully return a child to school, but be assured you have made a gigantic difference in that child's life. Success in life is often dictated by avoiding bad choices with irreversible consequences as well as tackling challenges that propel one to the next level or grade. One of the first young kids I treated for school refusal behavior is now in college. These are the kinds of cases that make all the effort worthwhile. Keep up the great work!

Appendix 1

Assessment Measures

School Refusal Assessment Scale–Revised (C)

Children sometimes have different reasons for not going to school. Some children feel bad at school, some have trouble with other people, some just want to be with their family, and others like to do things outside of school that are more fun.

This form asks questions about why you don't want to go to school. For each question, pick one number that describes you best for the last few days. After you answer one question, go on to the next. Don't skip any questions.

There are no right or wrong answers. Just pick the number that best fits the way you feel about going to school. Circle the number.

Here is an example of how it works. Try it. Circle the number that describes you *best.*

Example:
How often do you like to go shopping?

Never	Seldom	Sometimes	Half the Time	Usually	Almost Always	Always
0	1	2	3	4	5	6

Now go to the next page and begin to answer the questions.

School Refusal Assessment Scale–revised (C)

Name: _____

Age: _____

Date: _____

Please circle the answer that best fits the following questions:

1. How often do you have bad feelings about going to school because you are afraid of something related to school (for example, tests, school bus, teacher, fire alarm)?

Never	Seldom	Sometimes	Half the Time	Usually	Almost Always	Always
0	1	2	3	4	5	6

2. How often do you stay away from school because it is hard to speak with the other kids at school?

Never	Seldom	Sometimes	Half the Time	Usually	Almost Always	Always
0	1	2	3	4	5	6

3. How often do you feel you would rather be with your parents than go to school?

Never	Seldom	Sometimes	Half the Time	Usually	Almost Always	Always
0	1	2	3	4	5	6

4. When you are not in school during the week (Monday to Friday), how often do you leave the house and do something fun?

Never	Seldom	Sometimes	Half the Time	Usually	Almost Always	Always
0	1	2	3	4	5	6

5. How often do you stay away from school because you will feel sad or depressed if you go?

Never	Seldom	Sometimes	Half the Time	Usually	Almost Always	Always
0	1	2	3	4	5	6

6. How often do you stay away from school because you feel embarrassed in front of other people at school?

Never	Seldom	Sometimes	Half the Time	Usually	Almost Always	Always
0	1	2	3	4	5	6

7. How often do you think about your parents or family when in school?

Never	Seldom	Sometimes	Half the Time	Usually	Almost Always	Always
0	1	2	3	4	5	6

8. When you are not in school during the week (Monday to Friday), how often do you talk to or see other people (other than your family)?

Never	Seldom	Sometimes	Half the Time	Usually	Almost Always	Always
0	1	2	3	4	5	6

9. How often do you feel worse at school (for example, scared, nervous, or sad) compared to how you feel at home with friends?

Never	Seldom	Sometimes	Half the Time	Usually	Almost Always	Always
0	1	2	3	4	5	6

10. How often do you stay away from school because you do not have many friends there?

Never	Seldom	Sometimes	Half the Time	Usually	Almost Always	Always
0	1	2	3	4	5	6

11. How much would you rather be with your family than go to school?

Never	Seldom	Sometimes	Half the Time	Usually	Almost Always	Always
0	1	2	3	4	5	6

12. When you are not in school during the week (Monday to Friday), how much do you enjoy doing different things (for example, being with friends, going places)?

Never	Seldom	Sometimes	Half the Time	Usually	Almost Always	Always
0	1	2	3	4	5	6

13. How often do you have bad feelings about school (for example, scared, nervous, or sad) when you think about school on Saturday and Sunday?

Never	Seldom	Sometimes	Half the Time	Usually	Almost Always	Always
0	1	2	3	4	5	6

14. How often do you stay away from certain places in school (e.g., hallways, places where certain groups of people are) where you would have to talk to someone?

Never	Seldom	Sometimes	Half the Time	Usually	Almost Always	Always
0	1	2	3	4	5	6

15. How much would you rather be taught by your parents at home than by your teacher at school?

Never	Seldom	Sometimes	Half the Time	Usually	Almost Always	Always
0	1	2	3	4	5	6

16. How often do you refuse to go to school because you want to have fun outside of school?

Never	Seldom	Sometimes	Half the Time	Usually	Almost Always	Always
0	1	2	3	4	5	6

17. If you had fewer bad feelings (for example, scared, nervous, sad) about school, would it be easier for you to go to school?

Never	Seldom	Sometimes	Half the Time	Usually	Almost Always	Always
0	1	2	3	4	5	6

18. If it were easier for you to make new friends, would it be easier for you to go to school?

Never	Seldom	Sometimes	Half the Time	Usually	Almost Always	Always
0	1	2	3	4	5	6

19. Would it be easier for you to go to school if your parents went with you?

Never	Seldom	Sometimes	Half the Time	Usually	Almost Always	Always
0	1	2	3	4	5	6

20. Would it be easier for you to go to school if you could do more things you like to do after school hours (for example, being with friends)?

			Half the		Almost	
Never	Seldom	Sometimes	Time	Usually	Always	Always
0	1	2	3	4	5	6

21. How much more do you have bad feelings about school (for example, scared, nervous, or sad) compared to other kids your age?

			Half the		Almost	
Never	Seldom	Sometimes	Time	Usually	Always	Always
0	1	2	3	4	5	6

22. How often do you stay away from people at school compared to other kids your age?

			Half the		Almost	
Never	Seldom	Sometimes	Time	Usually	Always	Always
0	1	2	3	4	5	6

23. Would you like to be home with your parents more than other kids your age would?

			Half the		Almost	
Never	Seldom	Sometimes	Time	Usually	Always	Always
0	1	2	3	4	5	6

24. Would you rather be doing fun things outside of school more than most kids your age?

			Half the		Almost	
Never	Seldom	Sometimes	Time	Usually	Always	Always
0	1	2	3	4	5	6

Do not write below this line

1. _____	2. _____	3. _____	4. _____
5. _____	6. _____	7. _____	8. _____
9. _____	10. _____	11. _____	12. _____
13. _____	14. _____	15. _____	16. _____
17. _____	18. _____	19. _____	20. _____
21. _____	22. _____	23. _____	24. _____

Total
Score = _____   _____   _____   _____

Mean
Score = _____   _____   _____   _____

Relative
Ranking

  =   _____   _____   _____   _____

School Refusal Assessment Scale (P)

Name: _____

Date: _____

Please circle the answer that best fits the following questions:

1. How often does your child have bad feelings about going to school because he/she is afraid of something related to school (for example, tests, school bus, teacher, fire alarm)?

Never	Seldom	Sometimes	Half the Time	Usually	Almost Always	Always
0	1	2	3	4	5	6

2. How often does your child stay away from school because it is hard for him/her to speak with the other kids at school?

Never	Seldom	Sometimes	Half the Time	Usually	Almost Always	Always
0	1	2	3	4	5	6

3. How often does your child feel he/she would rather be with you or your spouse than go to school?

Never	Seldom	Sometimes	Half the Time	Usually	Almost Always	Always
0	1	2	3	4	5	6

4. When your child is not in school during the week (Monday to Friday), how often does he/she leave the house and do something fun?

Never	Seldom	Sometimes	Half the Time	Usually	Almost Always	Always
0	1	2	3	4	5	6

5. How often does your child stay away from school because he/she will feel sad or depressed if he/she goes?

Never	Seldom	Sometimes	Half the Time	Usually	Almost Always	Always
0	1	2	3	4	5	6

6. How often does your child stay away from school because he/she feels embarrassed in front of other people at school?

Never	Seldom	Sometimes	Half the Time	Usually	Almost Always	Always
0	1	2	3	4	5	6

7. How often does your child think about you or your spouse or family when in school?

			Half the		Almost	
Never	Seldom	Sometimes	Time	Usually	Always	Always
0	1	2	3	4	5	6

8. When your child is not in school during the week (Monday to Friday), how often does he/she talk to or see other people (other than his/her family)?

			Half the		Almost	
Never	Seldom	Sometimes	Time	Usually	Always	Always
0	1	2	3	4	5	6

9. How often does your child feel worse at school (for example, scared, nervous, or sad) compared to how he/she feels at home with friends?

			Half the		Almost	
Never	Seldom	Sometimes	Time	Usually	Always	Always
0	1	2	3	4	5	6

10. How often does your child stay away from school because he/she does not have many friends there?

			Half the		Almost	
Never	Seldom	Sometimes	Time	Usually	Always	Always
0	1	2	3	4	5	6

11. How much would your child rather be with his/her family than go to school?

			Half the		Almost	
Never	Seldom	Sometimes	Time	Usually	Always	Always
0	1	2	3	4	5	6

12. When your child is not in school during the week (Monday to Friday), how much does he/she enjoy doing different things (for example, being with friends, going places)?

Never	Seldom	Sometimes	Half the Time	Usually	Almost Always	Always
0	1	2	3	4	5	6

13. How often does your child have bad feelings about school (for example, scared, nervous, or sad) when he/she thinks about school on Saturday and Sunday?

Never	Seldom	Sometimes	Half the Time	Usually	Almost Always	Always
0	1	2	3	4	5	6

14. How often does your child stay away from certain places in school (e.g., hallways, places where certain groups of people are) where he/she would have to talk to someone?

Never	Seldom	Sometimes	Half the Time	Usually	Almost Always	Always
0	1	2	3	4	5	6

15. How much would your child rather be taught by you or your spouse at home than by his/her teacher at school?

Never	Seldom	Sometimes	Half the Time	Usually	Almost Always	Always
0	1	2	3	4	5	6

16. How often does your child refuse to go to school because he/she wants to have fun outside of school?

Never	Seldom	Sometimes	Half the Time	Usually	Almost Always	Always
0	1	2	3	4	5	6

17. If your child had fewer bad feelings (for example, scared, nervous, sad) about school, would it be easier for him/her to go to school?

			Half the		Almost	
Never	Seldom	Sometimes	Time	Usually	Always	Always
0	1	2	3	4	5	6

18. If it were easier for your child to make new friends, would it be easier for him/her to go to school?

			Half the		Almost	
Never	Seldom	Sometimes	Time	Usually	Always	Always
0	1	2	3	4	5	6

19. Would it be easier for your child to go to school if you or your spouse went with him/her?

			Half the		Almost	
Never	Seldom	Sometimes	Time	Usually	Always	Always
0	1	2	3	4	5	6

20. Would it be easier for your child to go to school if he/she could do more things he/she likes to do after school hours (for example, being with friends)?

			Half the		Almost	
Never	Seldom	Sometimes	Time	Usually	Always	Always
0	1	2	3	4	5	6

21. How much more does your child have bad feelings about school (for example, scared, nervous, or sad) compared to other kids his/her age?

			Half the		Almost	
Never	Seldom	Sometimes	Time	Usually	Always	Always
0	1	2	3	4	5	6

22. How often does your child stay away from people at school compared to other kids his/her age?

			Half the		Almost	
Never	Seldom	Sometimes	Time	Usually	Always	Always
0	1	2	3	4	5	6

23. Would your child like to be home with you or your spouse more than other kids his/her age would?

			Half the		Almost	
Never	Seldom	Sometimes	Time	Usually	Always	Always
0	1	2	3	4	5	6

24. Would your child rather be doing fun things outside of school more than most kids his/her age?

			Half the		Almost	
Never	Seldom	Sometimes	Time	Usually	Always	Always
0	1	2	3	4	5	6

Do not write below this line

1. _____	2. _____	3. _____	4. _____
5. _____	6. _____	7. _____	8. _____
9. _____	10. _____	11. _____	12. _____
13. _____	14. _____	15. _____	16. _____
17. _____	18. _____	19. _____	20. _____
21. _____	22. _____	23. _____	24. _____

Total
Score =   _____   _____   _____   _____

Mean
Score =   _____   _____   _____   _____

Relative
Ranking

=   _____   _____   _____   _____

Appendix 2

Readings and Additional Resources

Information Regarding Measures Described in Chapter 2

Child Behavior Checklist and Teacher's Report Form (Achenbach System of Empirically Based Assessment, www.aseba.org)

Child Symptom Inventory-4 (Western Psychological Services, www.wps publish.com)

Children's Depression Inventory (Multi-Health Systems, www.mhs.com)

Conners Rating Scales (Multi-Health Systems, www.mhs.com)

Multidimensional Anxiety Scale for Children (Multi-Health Systems, www.mhs.com)

Screen for Child Anxiety-Related Disorders (from author Boris Birmaher, Department of Psychiatry, Western Psychiatric Institute and Clinic, Pittsburg, PA)

Social Anxiety Scale for Children–Revised and Social Anxiety Scale for Adolescents (from author Annette La Greca: *Social anxiety scales for children and adolescents: Manual and instructions for the SASC, SASC-R, and SAS-A (adolescents), and parent versions of the scales.* Department of Psychology, University of Miami, Miami, FL).

Social Phobia and Anxiety Inventory for Children (Multi-Health Systems, www.mhs.com)

Additional Readings and Resources

If you are interested in reading additional material about the nature, cause, assessment, and treatment of school refusal behavior in youths, you may wish to examine the following list of books, book chapters, and journal articles that I and others have written about youths with school refusal behavior. Please refer to the website www.oup.com/us/schoolrefusal for updates over time.

Kearney, C. A. (in press). School absenteeism and school refusal behavior: A review of contemporary literature. *Clinical Psychology Review.*

Kearney, C. A. (2007). *Getting your child to say "yes" to school: A guide for parents of youth with school refusal behavior.* New York: Oxford University Press.

Kearney, C. A., & Albano, A. M. (2007). *When children refuse school: A cognitive-behavioral therapy approach/Parent workbook.* New York: Oxford University Press.

Kearney, C. A., & Albano, A. M. (2007). *When children refuse school: A cognitive-behavioral therapy approach/Therapist guide.* New York: Oxford University Press.

Kearney, C. A. (2006). Confirmatory factor analysis of the School Refusal Assessment Scale–Revised: Child and parent versions. *Journal of Psychopathology and Behavioral Assessment, 28,* 139–144.

Kearney, C. A., & Bensaheb, A. (2006). School absenteeism and school refusal behavior: A review and suggestions for school-based health professionals. *Journal of School Health, 76,* 1–5.

Kearney, C. A., Lemos, A., & Silverman, J. (2006). School refusal behavior. In R. B. Mennuti, A. Freeman, & R. W. Christner (Eds.), *Cognitive-behavioral interventions in educational settings: A handbook for practice* (pp. 89–105). New York: Brunner-Routledge.

Kearney, C. A., & Bates, M. (2005). Addressing school refusal behavior: Suggestions for frontline professionals. *Children and Schools, 27,* 207–216.

Kearney, C. A., Chapman, G., & Cook, L. C. (2005). Moving from assessment to treatment of school refusal behavior in youth. *International Journal of Behavioral and Consultation Therapy, 1,* 46–51.

Kearney, C. A., Chapman, G., & Cook, L. C. (2005). School refusal behavior in young children. *International Journal of Behavioral and Consultation Therapy, 1,* 212–218.

Kearney, C. A. (2004). Absenteeism. In T. S. Watson & C. H. Skinner (Eds.), *Encyclopedia of school psychology* (pp. 1–2). New York: Kluwer Academic/Plenum.

Kearney, C. A. (2004). School refusal. In T. S. Watson & C. H. Skinner (Eds.), *Encyclopedia of school psychology* (pp. 274–276). New York: Kluwer Academic/ Plenum.

Kearney, C. A. (2004). School refusal behavior. In W. E. Craighead & C. B. Nemeroff (Eds.), *The concise corsini encyclopedia of psychology and behavioral science* (3rd. ed., pp. 851–852). New York: Wiley.

Kearney, C. A., & Albano, A. M. (2004). The functional profiles of school refusal behavior: Diagnostic aspects. *Behavior Modification, 28,* 147–161.

Kearney, C. A., & Alvarez, K. M. (2004). Manualized treatment for school-refusal behavior in youth. In L. L'Abate (Ed.), *Using workbooks in mental health: Resources in prevention, psychotherapy, and rehabilitation for clinicians and researchers* (pp. 283–299). New York: Haworth.

Kearney, C. A., Lemos, A., & Silverman, J. (2004). The functional assessment of school refusal behavior. *The Behavior Analyst Today, 5,* 275–283.

Kearney, C. A. (2003). Bridging the gap among professionals who address youth with school absenteeism: Overview and suggestions for consensus. *Professional Psychology: Research and Practice, 34,* 57–65.

Kearney, C. A., Sims, K. E., Pursell, C. R., & Tillotson, C. A. (2003). Separation anxiety disorder in young children: A longitudinal and family analysis. *Journal of Clinical Child and Adolescent Psychology, 32,* 593–598.

Kearney, C. A. (2002). Case study of the assessment and treatment of a youth with multifunction school refusal behavior. *Clinical Case Studies, 1,* 67–80.

Kearney, C. A. (2002). Identifying the function of school refusal behavior: A revision of the School Refusal Assessment Scale. *Journal of Psychopathology and Behavioral Assessment, 24,* 235–245.

Kearney, C. A. (2001). *School refusal behavior in youth: A functional approach to assessment and treatment.* Washington, DC: American Psychological Association.

Kearney, C. A., Pursell, C., & Alvarez, K. (2001). Treatment of school refusal behavior in children with mixed functional profiles. *Cognitive and Behavioral Practice, 8,* 3–11.

Kearney, C. A., & Albano, A. M. (2000). *When children refuse school: A cognitive-behavioral therapy approach/Parent workbook.* San Antonio, TX/New York: The Psychological Corporation/Oxford University Press.

Kearney, C. A., & Albano, A. M. (2000). *When children refuse school: A cognitive-behavioral therapy approach/Therapist's guide.* San Antonio, TX/New York: The Psychological Corporation/Oxford University Press.

Kearney, C. A., & Hugelshofer, D. (2000). Systemic and clinical strategies for preventing school refusal behavior in youth. *Journal of Cognitive Psychotherapy, 14,* 51–65.

Kearney, C. A., & Pursell, C. (2000). School stress and school refusal behavior. In G. Fink (Ed.), *Encyclopedia of stress* (Vol. 3, pp. 398–402). San Diego, CA: Academic Press.

Kearney, C. A., & Silverman, W. K. (1999). Functionally-based prescriptive and nonprescriptive treatment for children and adolescents with school refusal behavior. *Behavior Therapy, 30,* 673–695.

Kearney, C. A., & Mizrachi, R. (1998). Interventions with school refusal behavior. In D. A. Sabatino & B. L. Brooks (Eds.), *Contemporary interdisciplinary interventions for children with emotional/ behavioral disorders* (pp. 247–265). Durham, NC: Carolina Academic Press.

Kearney, C. A., & Roblek, T. L. (1998). Parent training in the treatment of school refusal behavior. In J. M. Briesmeister & C. E. Schaefer (Eds.), *Handbook of parent training: Parents as co-therapists for children's behavior problems* (2nd. ed., pp. 225–256). New York: Wiley.

Kearney, C. A., & Tillotson, C. A. (1998). School attendance. In T. S. Watson & F. M. Gresham (Eds.), *Handbook of child behavior therapy* (pp. 143–161). New York: Plenum.

Kearney, C. A., & Tillotson, C. A. (1998). The School Refusal Assessment Scale. In C. P. Zalaquett & R. J. Wood (Eds.), *Evaluating stress: A book of resources* (Vol. 2, pp. 239–258). Lanham, MD: Scarecrow Press.

Kearney, C. A., & Sims, K. E. (1997). A clinical perspective on school refusal in youngsters. *In Session: Psychotherapy in Practice, 3,* 5–19.

Kearney, C. A., & Silverman, W. K. (1996). The evolution and reconciliation of taxonomic strategies for school refusal behavior. *Clinical Psychology: Science and Practice, 3,* 339–354.

Following is a list of other references regarding or related to school refusal behavior, including the systemic approaches discussed in Chapters 6–7:

Astor, R. A., Meyer, H. A., Benbenishty, R., Marachi, R., & Rosemond, M. (2005). School safety interventions: Best practices and programs. *Children and Schools, 27,* 17–32.

Barnet, B., Arroyo, C., Devoe, M., & Duggan, A.K. (2004). Reduced school dropout rates among adolescent mothers receiving school-based prenatal care. *Archives of Pediatric and Adolescent Medicine, 158,* 262–268.

Beidel, D.C., & Turner, S. M. (2005). *Childhood anxiety disorders: A guide to research and treatment.* New York: Routledge.

Broussard, C. A. (2003). Facilitating home-school partnerships for multiethnic families: School social workers collaborating for success. *Children and Schools, 25,* 211–222.

Eisen, A. R., & Schaefer, C. E. (2005). *Separation anxiety in children and adolescents: An individualized approach to assessment and treatment.* New York: Guilford.

Fantuzzo, J., Grim, S., & Hazan, H. (2005). Project Start: An evaluation of a community-wide school-based intervention to reduce truancy. *Psychology in the Schools, 42,* 657–667.

Garrison, A. H. (2006). "I missed the bus": School grade transition, the Wilmington Truancy Center, and reasons youth don't go to school. *Youth Violence and Juvenile Justice, 4,* 204–212.

Greene, M. B. (2005). Reducing violence and aggression in schools. *Trauma, Violence, and Abuse, 6,* 236–253.

Grolnick, W. S., Benjet, C., Kurowski, & Apostoleris, N. H. (1997). Predictors of parent involvement in children's schooling. *Journal of Educational Psychology, 89,* 538–548.

Hernandez, T. J., & Seem, S. R. (2004). A safe school climate: A systemic approach and the school counselor. *Professional School Counseling, 7,* 256–262.

Heyne, D., & Rollings, S. (2002). *School refusal.* Malden, MA: Blackwell.

Kearney, C. A. (2005). *Social anxiety and social phobia in youth: Characteristics, assessment, and psychological treatment.* New York: Springer.

Lever, N., Sander, M. A., Lombardo, S., Randall, C., Axelrod, J., Rubenstein, M., & Weist, M. D. (2004). A drop-out prevention program for high-risk inner-city youth. *Behavior Modification, 28,* 513–527.

McCluskey, C. P., Bynum, T. S., & Patchin, J. W. (2004). Reducing chronic absenteeism: An assessment of an early truancy initiative. *Crime and Delinquency, 50,* 214–234.

McWhirter, J. J., McWhirter, B. T., McWhirter, A.M., & McWhirter, E. H. (1998). *At-risk youth: A comprehensive response* (2nd ed.). Pacific Grove, CA: Brooks/Cole.

Morris, T. L., & March, J. S. (2004). *Anxiety disorders in children and adolescents* (2nd ed.). New York: Guilford.

Mytton, J. A., DiGuiseppi, Gough, D. A., Taylor, R. S., & Logan, S. (2002). School-based violence prevention programs: Systematic review of secondary prevention trials. *Archives of Pediatric and Adolescent Medicine, 156,* 752–762.

National Center for Education Statistics. (2006). *The condition of education 2006.* Washington, DC: U.S. Department of Education.

Ollendick, T. H., & Cerny, J. A. (1981). *Clinical behavior therapy with children.* New York: Plenum (now Springer).

Ollendick, T. H., & March, J. S. (2004). *Phobic and anxiety disorders in children and adolescents: A clinician's guide to effective psychosocial and pharmacological interventions.* New York: Oxford University Press.

Orfield, G. (Ed.). (2004). *Dropouts in America: Confronting the graduation rate crisis.* Cambridge, MA: Harvard Education Press.

Reid, K. (2003). A strategic approach to tackling school absenteeism and truancy: The PSCC scheme. *Educational Studies, 29,* 351–371.

Reid, K. (2003). The search for solutions to truancy and other forms of school absenteeism. *Pastoral Care, 21,* 3–9.

Reid, K. (2007). The views of learning mentors on the management of school attendance. *Mentoring and Tutoring, 15,* 39–55.

Reynolds, A. J., Temple, J. A., Robertson, D. L., & Mann, E. A. (2001). Long-term effects of an early childhood intervention on educational achievement and juvenile arrest: A 15-year follow-up of low-income children in public schools. *Journal of the American Medical Association, 285,* 2339–2346.

Schoenfelt, E. L., & Huddleston, M. R. (2006). The Truancy Court Diversion Program of the Family Court, Warren Circuit Court Division III, Bowling Green, Kentucky: An evaluation of impact on attendance and academic performance. *Family Court Review, 44,* 683–695.

Scott, D. M., & Friedli, D. (2002). Attendance problems and disciplinary procedures in Nebraska schools. *Journal of Drug Education, 32,* 149–165.

Silverman, W. K., & Kurtines, W. M. (1996). *Anxiety and phobic disorders: A pragmatic approach.* New York: Plenum (now Springer).

Silverman, W. K., & Treffers, P. D. A. (2001). *Anxiety disorders in children and adolescents: Research, assessment and intervention.* New York: Cambridge University Press.

Smith, P. K., Ananiadou, K., & Cowie, H. (2003). Interventions to reduce school bullying. *Canadian Journal of Psychiatry, 48,* 591–599.

Stone, S. (2006). Correlates of change in student reported parent involvement in schooling: A new look at the National Education

Longitudinal Study of 1988. *American Journal of Orthopsychiatry, 76,* 518–530.

Vreeman, R. C., & Carroll, A. E. (2007). A systematic review of school-based interventions to prevent bullying. *Archives of Pediatric and Adolescent Medicine, 161,* 78–88.

White, M. D., Fyfe, J. J., Campbell, S. P., & Goldkamp, J. S. (2001). The school-police partnership: Identifying at-risk youth through a truant recovery program. *Evaluation Review, 25,* 507–532.

Woody, D. (2001). A comprehensive school-based conflict-resolution model. *Children and Schools, 23,* 115–123.

Worrell, F. C., & Hale, R. L. (2001). The relationship of hope in the future and perceived school climate to school completion. *School Psychology Quarterly, 16,* 370–388.